APPROACHING THEOLOGY

*Asking the Right Questions
Enables the Best Answers*

Barry L. Callen

Emeth Press
www.emethpress.com

APPROACHING THEOLOGY
Asking the Right Questions Enables the Best Answers

Copyright © 2015 Barry L. Callen
Printed in the United States of America on acid-free paper

All rights reserved. No part of this book may be reproduced, or stored in a retrieval system or transmitted in any form or by any means, electronic, mechanical, photocopying, recording, scanning or otherwise, except as permitted by the 1976 United States Copyright Act, or with the prior written permission of Emeth Press. Requests for permission should be addressed to: Emeth Press, P. O. Box 23961, Lexington, KY 40523-3961.   http://www.emethpress.com.

Library of Congress Cataloging-in-Publication Data

Callen, Barry L.
  Approaching theology : asking the right questions enables the best answers / Barry L. Callen.
      pages cm
   ISBN 978-1-906470-92-0 (alk. paper)
   1. Theology. I. Title.
   BR118.C3225 2015
   230--dc23
                              2014049502

CONTENTS

Preface / v

1. Access to the Teacher / 1

2. Theorizing or Tasting? / 9

3. The Opening Questions / 17

4. Hanging Three Pictures / 25

5. Land of the Corpses / 33

6. A Deadly Duo / 43

7. God's Grace Grammar / 51

8. Back to the Basics / 59

9. Fixed and Fluid / 69

10. But Which Is Which? / 79

11. The Essential Nouns / 87

12. The Essential Verbs / 99

13. Bench Players / 113

14. The End Is the Beginning / 127

15. Endnotes / 135

Preface

You now are stepping into the world of Christian theology. My task is to help you walk carefully, in part by highlighting the right questions and guiding you toward the best answers. This is not a "systematic" theology book. It does not address every theological subject nor give a full explanation to every theological topic. For you, that might come later. But for now, as you begin the theological journey, other things should come first.

I admit it—and I know it sounds a little intellectual and stuffy, but it's the truth. For decades I functioned as the editor of more than one organization publishing academic materials in the field of Christian theology. I've worked with sophisticated scholars and handled hundreds of their intellectual articles and thousands of their detailed footnotes. At the banquet when my editorship of the *Wesleyan Theological Journal* was concluding and being celebrated, I was given a beautiful plaque. It said that I had "eruditiously facilitated" the development of the journal during my years. It might have read "wisely helped" or "thoughtfully guided," but the bigger and more obscure words were chosen by some sophisticated and well-meaning writer.

That's often how it is in the world of Christian theology. Please don't misunderstand me. I am proud of my intellectual work. I am grateful for positive and appreciative words tossed my way, however big they are. Intellectual inquiry of the highest sort is valuable to the life of the church. Even so, words should be chosen to fit the audience—and we're not all "intellectuals." Maybe you're not one, at least not yet.

I admire—and wish to reflect in this book—the stance of William Barclay. He was a fine biblical scholar from Scotland who wrote commentaries on the books of the New Testament. They have been read and loved by countless Christians of recent generations. Despite his great learning, Barclay never aspired to be an "ivory-tower" academic. He could see little purpose in a belief system so wrapped up in complicated words that it was accessible only to "experts." The sad fact is that, for many believers, Christian theology is wrapped up that way. I trust that what I write here is more of the Barclay style.

"Erudition" is not what I admire most, even though a form of this word got on a plaque that I treasure. As you read here, you can relax and put your dictionary away. Yes, there are a few endnotes in the back of this book. They are there in part so that you'll know that I haven't made everything up from scratch. But you can ignore them if you want—unless, of course, this book is being used as a class textbook and your professor has told you to do otherwise.

Here's what I'm up to in these pages. Let me explain by borrowing two sentences from the review of a book titled *The Pursuit of Happiness* that appears in the spring 2014 issue of the *Wesleyan Theological Journal*:

> The expert reader will see both the rigor of her thought and the complexity of the issues she discusses, but the novice will encounter few stumbling blocks to an introductory understanding of those same issues.... Plain speaking need not be antithetical to thoughtful scholarship.

Well said. I'm for plain speaking even when the subject is big and complex. As you read, I hope you encounter the real issues in Christian theology, issues made accessible to any "novice" who needs an "introductory understanding."

There's no shame in starting at the beginning. I realize that you may be extraordinary in many ways, just not (yet) in the complicated world of Christian theology. Since you're entering the this world, I'm determined to assist—and without placing in front of you unnecessary stumbling blocks that make things harder than they have to be. Writing about theology in plain language, but without distorting the subject in the process, is is a tough task, but you're worth it!

Know this. Everything in print, even if understandable, is hardly worth taking seriously. For instance, a little book is titled *The Devil's Dictionary*. Why is it frequently stolen from public libraries? For one thing, its title suggests that it's more than it actually is (Ambrose Bierce and not the Devil is the author). Bierce defines "dictionary" as a "malevolent literary device for cramping the growth of a language and making it hard and inelastic." By contrast, he speaks proudly of his own little dictionary as "a most useful work." Why? Because his definitions are soft and expansive, really just plain sarcastic. The word "Revelation" gets this fresh definition: "A famous book in which St. John the Divine concealed all that he knew. The revealing is done by the commentators, who know nothing."

Theologians have been accused of doing that too, claiming more than they really know and hiding their ignorance inside words hard to pronounce. While not always guilty as accused, the stereotype certainly lives on. I want to be innocent of this. I want to author no graffiti such as this that appeared on a university wall:

Jesus said unto them: "Who do you say that I am?"

And they replied: "You are the eschatological manifestation of the ground of our being, the kerygma in which we find the ultimate meaning of our interpersonal relationships."

And Jesus said: "What?"

The task of this book is to guide you into the world of Christian theology by helping you ask the right questions, find the best answers, and avoid the typical pitfalls along the way—and in language that Jesus and you can both understand.

1
ACCESS TO THE TEACHER

Question: What is the task of theology and who is the primary teacher?

I taught in a Christian university for a long time. We justified the cost to students of such education by noting several facts that make a quality difference. One was that, unlike some institutions with huge classes taught by graduate students, we had relatively small class sizes always taught by top professors who were accessible to students outside the classroom.

The identity of the teacher is very important, as it how available that teacher is for individual learning needs. When it comes to Christian theology, one must think first and foremost of Jesus Christ. When all is said and done, he is the heart of the matter.[1] He is both teacher and the primary subject bring taught. The promise is that his Spirit is assigned to every classroom of disciples in every time and place. Sitting at the feet of this divine teacher is quality theological education!

Having said at least that much, and before we get started, let's gain some broad perspective, and do it in an unusual way. Ready? Let's go back to the very beginning of the story of Jesus.

Joseph and Jesus

Do you remember that amazing New Testament story about the birth of Jesus? Who could have blamed Joseph if he had decided to have Mary humiliated in public—or worse. He had found out that she had become pregnant before they were married, and without his help. Even so, and despite the shock and sense of betrayal, he was gracious enough to plan a separation from her with a minimum of public disgrace that would ruin her whole life. But that wasn't the end of this story, or the whole of it, not even close!

Joseph learned something else, something that came to him out of the clouds somewhere, something that helped him go easy on Mary. He was told that the pregnancy was actually God's doing—however that could be. Before long King Herod caught the rumor that a new king was nearby and was starting to have babies killed in Bethlehem to get at Mary's little boy whom he feared was a political threat. No kid with divine credentials could be tolerated. So, like a protective and loving father, Joseph grabbed their few suitcases and scurried off to Egypt with Mary and the little Jesus, her (their) special baby. They would hide down there until the coast with clear--which meant seeing Herod's name appearing in an obituary column.

I need to say a little more about this business of Joseph receiving critical information from "right out of the clouds somewhere." The more traditional way of putting it is "an angel of the Lord appeared to him in a dream" (Matt. 1:20). There is a rich heritage of dream revelations in the Bible.[2] There also are two other things. One is a tendency over recent centuries to dismiss such revelations as more psychologically revealing of the dreamer than as possible messages from God. The other, reversing this negative tendency, is a more recent tendency to be open to the possible legitimacy of such things.

Today there are numerous scientists willing to go beyond a preoccupation with quarks and neutrons and return to wondering if there might be a clear pattern in the worlds as we are beginning to know them. There are new generations of thinkers more willing—even anxious—to seek life's wisdom in wonder, meditation, experience, beauty, intuition, incense, and love. They are ready to add to their telescopes and computers an embracing of the faith dimension of life and the meaningfulness of spiritual experience and insight as part of the larger knowing process. Despite all the "information" at hand, they are humbled, hearing Jesus inviting the children to his feet and accepting his announcement that God's kingdom might be something like that.

What follows in this book certainly does not abandon the past tradition of Christian believing, especially its biblical foundations. However, it is especially sensitive to the times in which we now live—theology always must do that. I will represent the fixed ideas of the biblical past as religious *nouns* and the more fluid styles of contemporary believing and expressing belief as religious *verbs*. We must know and affirm whatever is absolutely essential to be Christian, of course. But we also must *be* and *do* what such beliefs require and enable. Full Christian sentences must have the right subjects, verbs, and supporting tenses, adverbs, adjectives, etc. More on that later. Let's get back to Joseph.

When Matthew wrote his Gospel about the amazing life of Jesus, the lineage of this baby was traced back through Joseph's family line clear to Abraham (Matt. 1:1-17). Doing that made an important theological point for Jewish readers, and Christian theology is always involved in the story of Jesus that is rooted deeply in the Hebrew heritage. Luke's Gospel gives more attention to Mary in his reporting about the origins of Jesus. A favorite writer of mine once commented: "Since Jesus himself never seems to have much worried about theology, it is hard not to believe that. . .he would have preferred Luke's version."[3] Said the Master himself, in effect, "Thanks for everything, Dad, and thanks to Dr. Luke for giving Mom her just due."

Even though I also applaud Dr. Luke, I hesitate about the little comment that Jesus never worried much about theology. Wrong! It's true that he never wrote a theology book and never delivered heavy lectures in any of the hallowed halls of Roman, Greek, or Hebrew centers of learning. Even so, he had great theological concern about his people, his Father (not Joseph), and his own mission. He loved his rich Jewish tradition and said plainly that didn't intend to destroy it (Matt. 5:17). He worked hard at getting it straightened out, understood properly, fulfilling it, bringing it to new life for all the world. That's the work of theology at its best!

What constitutes theological work? Theology surely has as central functions embracing tradition, thinking it through for yourself, and bringing it to new life in a new place and time. Jesus wanted his Father (God) properly understood. He chided religious leaders who really weren't listening, and he spent most of his time with the common people who were much more ready to receive and rejoice in the truth that Jesus was bringing, and that he said *he was*.

In fact, at the center of Christian theology is who Jesus was (is) and not only what he taught. He was plain in his language, colorful and clear in his meaning, and finally plainest of all by speaking boldly with his very life, death, and resurrection--all of which became an argument for his amazing identity, an argument that is hard to ignore or finally rebut.

Jesus, Our Theologian

Jesus, a theologian? Oh, yes, the best! He delivered the Word of God from the heart of the Father, and in him that Word was an agent of transformation for the lives of hungry and hurting people. Jesus made plain the saving story of God who is with us for our highest good. He even declared that he *was* God with us for our salvation! We are warned against being comfortable with a rudimentary understanding of the word of God that is resident in Jesus. We are to move on to a more mature wisdom that is able to "distinguish good from evil" (Heb. 5:12, 14). Truly knowing Jesus and moving on to a more mature wisdom about what that means is to be doing Christian theology.

So, as we begin our theological adventure together, let's agree on several things. Let's thank both Joseph and Mary. Let's be plain in our language. Let's be cautious about our claims and humble in our attitudes. Let's look to Jesus as our gracious pioneer and guide, daring even to accept him as God with us. And let's bow before the throne of the Father God whose amazing story is what it's all about. It's the story that, through the ministry of Christ's Spirit and his people, is now reaching even you--us.

And one more thing—a really important thing. The theology business requires faith--sorry if you hoped for something a little easier that you might handle only in your head. Things well beyond us require stretching and risking—although, taking Jesus into account, faith has some real history behind it and some actual light coming over the horizon of our limited knowledge. It's faith, always, but not faith completely wandering in the dark.

Here's a little perspective that sheds valuable light. Let's take the top and bottom of world society from the time of Jesus--and give Mr. Buechner a positive stroke after I've questioned his anti-theology comment about Jesus. Buechner speaks of Caesar as having ruled the world of Jesus' time as a virtual god in many eyes. That was the very top. But today, except for a few history majors in college, Caesar tends to be remembered mostly because...

> At some point during his reign, in a rundown section of one of the more obscure imperial provinces, out behind a cheesy motel among cow flops and moldy hay, a child was born to a pair of up-country

rubes you could have sold the Brooklyn Bridge to without even trying.[4]

Herod took the birth of Jesus seriously for selfish reasons. Joseph and Mary, the up-country rubes, played their crucial roles, and then Jesus and his disciples proceeded to upset the world. So much for Herod; so much for Caesar.

Things aren't always what they appear. The bottom, the disarming birth of Jesus in a remote barn, may actually be the top, the Lord of lords and King of kings. It's hard to recognize God when he comes dressed in soiled diapers! Thanks, Joseph and Mary, for having faith long ago, for listening to angels, for taking an extended trip to Egypt, and for giving us a chance to know and be changed by your amazing little boy who now sits at God's right hand astride the eternities. Jesus became the greatest of all theologians, both interpreting, sharing, and actually being—enfleshing--God's truth in our world. Now we are going to try to learn how to be good theologians ourselves. Jesus will always be our model and his Spirit our best teacher.

The Pain of Parables

My hope is to agree with Jesus always--that is, if I can understand him! Sometimes the teaching style of the Master was particularly hard to master. He used surprises, satirical comments, and lots of little stories and parables with no immediately clear meaning to most hearers.

Imagine yourself listening to Jesus along the shore of the Sea of Galilee. He is in his little pulpit-boat a few yards out so that everybody can see and hear. He already has quite a reputation as someone amazingly different—likely what brought you to listen to him. You and the hundreds standing around you are anxious to absorb whatever wisdom from God is about to flow from his mouth. Then Jesus says this (Matt. 13:11-12), seemingly to his disciples in particular who are nearest him, but loud enough for everyone to hear:

> To you it has been given to know the secrets of the kingdom of heaven, but to them it has not been given. For to those who have, more will be given. . .but from those who have nothing, even what they have will be taken away.

What? He seems to be telling his inner circle of friends something fresh about kingdom secrets. Why secrets? He's announcing what sounds like really bad news. You and I, members of the mass of outsiders to the inner circle, don't get the secrets, he says. Worse yet, we will know even less when he's done with his teaching. Ouch! Is there any point in listening any more? Apparently the more we hear the less we'll understand! Is that what it feels like to be studying theology?

If we are hearing Jesus right, his sermon is dead on arrival. His evangelistic technique will go nowhere. We are outside real understanding and will be getting even farther away as time goes on. In fact, a significant group of early Christians came to hear Jesus in just this elitist way. The "Gnostics" understood him to mean that salvation comes through having a special spiritual knowledge (*gnosis*) that is available only to the church's inside believers, the spiritual elite. The rest of us must follow along blindly, having faith and walking in relative ignorance.

But is this the correct way to hear Jesus? Is theology that shrouded in mystery? Surely not, hopefully not. But if not, why did Jesus talk in riddles and parables and speak of spiritual secrets? Didn't he want us to understand? How can I agree with him if his meanings remain at arm's length from those of us who aren't spiritual specialists?

There are good answers to these questions, but they require careful biblical interpretation that's not our purpose here. The bottom line is that Jesus was *God with us*, the divine presence choosing to radiate reality to us through human flesh so that finally we could get a proper fix on who God really is and on what God is all about on our behalf. The intention of the "incarnation" (the enfleshing of God in Jesus) is that finally we *will understand*. Still, the dilemma remains. There are real obstacles to our spiritual understanding. Jesus knew that very well. He already was being opposed by many who didn't understand him—and maybe didn't want to. Maybe that's what he meant—those who turn a deaf ear his way will get deafer still.

Can we understand the things of God? That classic passage in Job 38 makes clear that God will never be totally known to us limited humans. God's depth and grandeur and power and goodness are ultimately incomprehensible to mere people like us. In some ways, even in the clearest light that shines from Jesus, God remains something of a holy mystery. Beyond this limiting fact, Jesus went on to identify more obstacles to our understanding. This theology business won't always be easy.

Jesus knew that circumstances were piled up against what he was trying to get across in his teaching. He was sorrowing that the crowd wasn't ready for the truth. They were driven by curiosity and many personal agendas. He was alerting them--and us--to our present inability to profit from his teaching without some personal change. The problem often is not the teacher, but the students.

One reason that some do not hear Jesus properly is that they have too much to lose and no intention of losing it. Especially for religious and political leaders in places of privilege, it was (and is?) a simple power issue. They were (are) threatened by Jesus and thus actively opposed his message and ministry. The rich young ruler was blocked from real understanding and change because of his excessive attachment to his riches (Lk. 18:18-25).

Then came from Jesus a troubling parable that points to still other problems. There once was a sower who placed good seeds in various settings. Jesus was making the point that the good news from God often falls on poor soil, or on good soil filled with complicating circumstances. For many people, possible persecution outweighs their willingness to hear and accept even a word from God. For others, believing happens but is quickly compromised by the invasion of the world's cares and seductions. And then there is one other problem—a big one according to Jesus. "The evil one comes and snatches away what is sown in the heart" (Matt. 13:19).

There is much that opposes in-depth understanding of the gracious word coming to us from God in Jesus Christ. Real understanding sometimes seems almost impossible for the average person in today's churches who hasn't been to seminary and isn't inside trained clergy circles. Are we, the ordinary believers, to be left on the outside of real understanding? Is in-depth spiritual knowledge reserved for only select disciples? No! Jesus came to clarify, to convey God's truth, to overcome the obstacles with waves of divine light and love.

Here is the best thing. Jesus, the primary teacher of theology and the center of the subject being taught, has promised this:

> I have said these things to you while I am still with you. But the Advocate, the Holy Spirit, whom the Father will send in my name, *will teach you everything*, and remind you of all that I have said to you.... Do not let your hearts be troubled, and do not let them be afraid. (Jn. 14:25-27)

We *can* understand; we *will* understand, at least understand everything essential for our lives and ministries and destinies. The big question is our openness to the ongoing teaching work of the Spirit of God.

2

THEORIZING OR TASTING?

*Question: What about this hostile world and
the many disturbing questions?*

A telescope has been defined sarcastically as a device having a relation to the eye similar to what a telephone has to the ear—enabling distant objects or voices to come close and plague us with a mass of needless and unwanted details. Sound like Facebook? Is theology the church's annoying telescope? Does it only overwhelm and confuse us?

Sorry, but it's hard to make theological things easy! A mass of strange words tends to come at us. I'm anxious to simplify without dumbing things down to the point of losing the integrity of what I'm saying. I take comfort in the fact that Jesus spoke the greatest truths in the simplest of stories.

I admit having the fear of being simplistic instead of simple. I worry about introducing you to Christian theology with nothing being accomplished in the end but you having walked through the water with me for miles and only getting your feet wet. On the other hand, what have we accomplished if you and I only get one-hundred yards together and you die in the deep water?

What Is Theology?

Putting things of great import in plain language that makes sense is a difficult and slippery business. Wish me luck. After all, I'm trying to do this for you. One way to get it done is to keep pointing beyond mere words. We will champion the ultimate wisdom found only in there being an actual relationship between each of us and the living and loving God. We will call for knees and brains, praying our hardest and thinking our best.

To really know in the world of Christian theology means more than having mastered a set of big words and complex thoughts. Sure, you'll have to study some, but maybe you will also have to be on your knees some. Theology is no ordinary subject. The irony is thick, I know. We must use words to point beyond mere words. In order to manage focusing more on the relational, dynamic, and life-changing, we will wind up making some doctrinal statements that can become cold and distant. The risk is inevitable.

We who seek to know, love, be changed by, and serve God must have some belief structure to support the whole business. We need some language with which to talk about God, share our faith in God, and explain to others why God in Jesus Christ is so important to us—and potentially to them. Our language for these things is our theology.

Did you catch the "be changed by"? Christian theology should be more than an "objective" study pursued out of a primarily academic interest. It speaks to our very beings and will never be truly understood and properly implemented if we are not open to the possibility of a dramatic change of our inner lives. The more academic pursuit is philosophy and the history of religions, and maybe the studying of the Bible only as a literary exercise—all of interest, but not what theology hopes to be and do.

Theology is a believer seeking greater understanding of the faith. It is the pursuit of God in light of God's prior pursuit of us. Got that? The being of God is assumed—we begin our "ology" work because we believe that "Theo" actually is and we need to know much more about that. The God who *is* also is understood to be *Self-revealed* to us. So, theology is about locating the revelation, gaining increased understanding of it, and putting it into a language that can be shared meaningfully with others. But theology is still more.

Beyond our minds, theological work involves allowing divine revelation to penetrate our very lives so that the best sharing we do with others becomes *ourselves* and not merely our best and treasured words. The language of theology is meaningful only when it comes from experience and leads to experience. Christian theology is more than a particular theory about the universe, more than thoughtful religious teaching written down and routinely repeated. It is a spiritual path we must be willing to travel.

Each novice theologian must verify in life what is captured in the creed. You and I must *re-live* the tradition of the teachers and disciples of past generations. God has no grandchildren. To be a generation removed from the reality is not to be alive at all. To probe and theorize about God may be good, but it is not good enough. As the psalmist says, we must *taste* to really know that the Lord is good (Psalm 34:8).

Confession or Confusion?

We all face an immediate problem. Today's world is filled with injustice, frustration, and skepticism. Things aren't right and we don't know what to do about it. The air we breathe today is thick with numerous beliefs and no belief (so the atheists think), and many people are convinced that it doesn't matter which way you go on the belief business as long as you stick quietly to your own commitments or lack of them and keep to yourself. Tolerance is king (or queen if you're gender sensitive). Don't bother others with your personal religious stuff. Live and let live. Believe and be quiet. After all, nobody knows for sure.

"Evangelism" has become virtually a swear word in the public arena. At least in the United States, the rule of thumb is that the public should not be exposed to the Ten Commandments of the Old Testament because just seeing them on public property might destroy religious even-handedness. Christianity should be a private set of unstructured, wholesome emotions, lots of fun events around the church, and good deeds done by well-meaning religious people. Getting theological about things only causes trouble.

Preachers can preach, of course, as long as there are no captive audiences or restrictive bottom lines that divide people. As truly modern and enlightened people, our official confession should be that we have none except the creed of neutrality that affirms the worth of everyone and the frailness of our own religious tradition.

And then there's that story—maybe more serious than you think—of the scary old basement. We start the tale with a question. What is a Christian theologian? Here's the answer given by those who are sure of nothing in the religious realm and suspicious of anyone who has any definite convictions. Ready for this little piece of cynical anti-theology? A theologian is someone who goes down the treacherous stairs of a big old house into a very dark basement. He or she is looking for an illusive black cat that *isn't there*—and, oh my, *finds it*! The anticipation dictates the result, regardless of reality.

Want to be a theologian? Have a flashlight handy? Whoever thinks the illusive cat actually has been found is most likely deluded—so goes the common cynicism of today. If one's reputation for sanity and humility is to remain, it is best to slip down those stairs alone with warm milk in hand and feed the little thing occasionally--and keep quiet about it. Should te milk accumulate and sour over time, the terrible truth will become obvious even to the supposed finder.

John Killinger once wrote a good little book on the Apostles' Creed.[5] This classic Christian statement of faith is likely the oldest and best-known expression of Christian belief, a compacted piece of core theology. It's a brief and brilliant confession of faith used worldwide even though some would say it's just black-cat talk. Killinger refers to a church woman not in touch with this creed or any other from her Christian faith tradition. She is blissfully theology-less. He wonders if she came into the church on a *"confusion* of faith" (instead of a "confession"). Is some theology necessary to be a good church member? Yes!

Many church people relate to their faith in this casual and theologically uninformed way. They aren't able or willing or to see the need to do much else. "I go to church and sing all the songs—who, by the way, took the hymnals? Isn't that enough?" Can we park our minds at the church door with our coats? Isn't theology the preacher's business? The rest of us are obligated only to show up, sing, put a little something in the plate each week, and try to love Jesus and our neighbors.

Let me be plain about this parking question. The answer is "No!" Going to church doesn't make one a Christian any more than going to McDonalds makes one a hamburger! The Pharisees put plenty in the temple treasury, but it was a woman with almost nothing to give who drew praise from Jesus (Lk. 21:1-4). Christianity is not, and never has been, merely about going to the right building on Sundays or giving particular amounts for church support or finding the right combination of words with which to claim faith.

What, then, is it? The faith called for by Jesus is mostly about encountering and being transformed by the living and loving and redeeming God made known in the Christ. It's life being changed and a new life being lived. The title and subtitle of one of my books is *Catch Your Breath! Exhaling Death and Inhaling Life*. If all that is to happen, some thoughtful words must be there to define and guide the process. The idea that "we can somehow worship, adore, and imitate Jesus Christ without developing doctrines about him is indefensible.... To fail to develop doctrines about Jesus Christ is to reveal a dangerously shallow commitment to him, and to the unremitting human quest for truth."[6]

I know that's a strong stance, but I see no viable choice that is truly biblical. "Doctrine"—the very word sends shivers down a lot of spines (although people who try to avoid theology hardly have much of a faith spine for shivers to travel down). The idea of doctrine conjures up images of hard-bitten theologians arguing pointlessly in some foreign language about who knows what minor point. Isn't that whole business irrelevant to practical life and likely a relic of a bygone age? This is a common question with a clear answer. No!

If I am enjoying the fellowship of the church house where I hang out, is it really important that I know whether or not there really is a cat in that basement? Does the basement business bother you? Are you willing to go down there? Is there a good flashlight available that would help you avoid falling in the dark? We are talking about the big faith risk. No one who always stays upstairs is likely to be convinced of any good basement news merely by your report that something is really down there. The same goes if you never go down. But if you do go down and really find something life-changing, and then neglect finding a way to talk about it meaningfully to others, you still have short-circuited the full task of being a Christian.

Theology covers much territory. More than abstract theorizing about big philosophic issues of life and death, it also must involve a life engagement that (1) *tastes* the truth affirmed, (2) *digests* the substance of this wonderful bread of life, and (3) *prepares* a compelling report of this engagement that attracts others to this gracious table of living water. We are to (1) find the truth (which first has found us), (2) be set free by it, and (3) learn to speak about our joy in clear ways that will draw others to the fountain of life from which we now drink.

Disturbing Personal Questions

Penetrating personal questions are in order, some very direct ones. Are you confused about some very big life issues and not satisfied with where you are in the upstairs of your life's house? The risk/challenge/opportunity being offered to you theologically is that go down to the basement foundation of things, be open to belief—consciously, deliberately, thoughtfully and not stupidly, belief that God *is*, that God is *truly good*, and that we should risk everything by *responding radically* to that love with the totality of our own lives.

Jesus said to sell everything for the sake of finding a true treasure somewhere in a faith field—or basement (Matt. 13:44). Are you ready to sell? Theology is about thinking carefully and putting your own life on the line by buying the most costly thing of all. Theology can be a frustrating and pointless subject if you are determined not to change, not to risk in faith, not to think hard about large matters.

The kingdom of God, if it is at all, is hidden in the field of life as it is. Finding it and following through with your heart, head, and mouth is the stuff of Christian theology. Doing theology (and being a good disciple of Jesus) involves getting to the right spot in the field (basement), learning where you are when you arrive, recognizing the treasure when you see it, and figuring out how best to understand that kingdom treasure and share its great worth with others.

If you do find life's great treasure, word of the find must not be hidden. Effective sharing will demand that you witness well to others on their own turf and in their own terms. Being a credible witness requires that you be changed by what you find--by the God who has graciously found you. The change must be obvious in a love that is hard to explain except that you actually have tapped into the eternal kingdom of love.

Want to Be a Theologian?

Did you get all of that? Still want to be a theologian? If you intend to be a serious Christian, the answer must be "yes!" We are all called by Jesus to be field hunters, basement goers, treasure finders, and good news spreaders. If Jesus really was raised from the dead, we must reflect on that, grasp what it means, put it into plain and wonder-full words, and then embody with our very lives the special living that it makes possible.

Christianity is not only nice feelings about loving other people. It also is a way of understanding all of reality and of defining what is proper, moral, important, and possible, now and hereafter. Even more, it must embody the good news of the yet-coming and already-arriving reign of God (see much more on this in the last chapter).

Confused about the biggest of life issues? Dissatisfied with your confusion? Interested in a change? Will you dare to risk everything on a faith journey? Are you ready to get past a mere "confusion" of faith? Killinger's little book is titled *You Are What You Believe*. If you're not clear about your belief, apparently you don't know who you really are--and still could be. If you are ready to move from that sad situation, then let's get going on the theological journey!

I realize that you may have been confused or hurt by believers or congregations of Christians you have known up close. Unfortunately, there are many confusing messages announced in our churches. You may identify painfully with the accidental message conveyed on a church sign (we'll refrain from naming the place). The sign said: "Don't Let Worries Kill You. Let the Church Help!" One church bulletin read, innocently enough: "The peacemaking meeting scheduled for today has been cancelled due to a conflict." Another reminded the church folks of the coming conference on prayer and fasting, adding: "The cost for attending includes meals." Still another announced that the evening sermon would be "What is Hell?" and awkwardly added, "Come early and listen to our choir practice."

You may worry that trying the theology thing is little more than speculating about imponderables in the service of one's own personal needs and ends. One of the greatest of Christian theologians really upset the church's establishment in the sixteenth century. Martin Luther launched the Protestant Reformation and reshaped the future that is still with us. One of his biographers noted his personal struggle in adult life with constipation and wondered something a bit off the wall. Might this giant of a thinker have been more satisfied with the church's status quo if he'd had access to a good laxative? Is doing theology just an exercise in formulating beliefs that meet our felt needs and fulfill our own agendas and quite our personal frustrations?

Remember *The Devil's Dictionary*? In it Ambrose Bierce suggests something a bit indelicate. He says that "indigestion" is sometimes mistaken for deep religious conviction. Then he quotes a "simple Red Man of the western wild" who supposedly once said: "Plenty well, no pray; big bellyache, heap God."[7] Yes, we people are failing bodies with swirling emotions and unanswered questions. We tend to turn to God only when in a heap of trouble. So, is theology merely the result of all such incidental and ultimately meaningless things? I hope not—I believe not.

How about one more bit of perspective? Theology is very important, but not the ultimate thing in the Christian life. Let me share a plain-language story that puts theology where it belongs. A Roman centurion once came to Jesus. This military man had much power at his command. Nonetheless, he came humbly to a Jewish teacher, asking Jesus for a big personal favor—quite the reversal of usual identities and roles. Likely, this privileged Roman military man knew little of the religious thinking of the Jews. What he had come to know somehow was that a word from the mouth of Jesus could accomplish for an ailing servant what his own heavily armed men of Rome could not get done.

The point is this. Knowing theology is important for Christians, but not supremely important. This centurion, ignorant of the details of Jewish theology, still knew something of overarching importance. As Martin Luther once said, "faith is a living, bold trust in God's grace." What was the reaction of Jesus to this surprising faith of a theologically unlettered Roman man? According to Matthew 8, he spoke the needed healing word and then went on to shockingly announce that people of faith like the centurion will make it to heaven faster than lots of sophisticated and polished "religious" folks. Plain enough? Know your theology, definitely; never forget, however, who is Lord and where the power is!

Even with all the problems and miscommunications in church life, and with proper cautions in place, will you stay open, searching, and trusting? Come along with me on this theological journey. We'll start with a tent, a song, and a barn—all on our way down into the basement where the great treasure may be waiting. Can you handle this? I'll be careful about what signs we stick out on the church lawn. I'll try to use only words that convey what we really mean to say, ones that don't drive you to the dictionary.

3

THE OPENING QUESTIONS

Questions: Is it important to start with the right questions? If so, what are they?

Here is a wrong question with which to begin theologically. "If I study theology carefully, will I finally manage to get all of the answers to life's questions?" This answer to this is easy. "No!" You will have gained much, but never all the answers. Beware of the arrogant person who claims wisdom greater than everyone else. You always will have to live with some lack of clarity, even some doubt. Why does one person suffer and not another? If God is truly good and all-powerful, why does anyone ever suffer? Exactly when will Jesus return? Is the Israel of today the true people of God? Will there be any Hindus in heaven?

Many such questions will get only partial answers in the best of theological systems. Be ready for that. Theology is more than inheriting a polished set of clear answers to everything we would like to know for sure.

The Right Opening Questions

Before actually engaging in direct theological work, there is some water to wade through. My job is to guide you so that you won't step in the wrong place and have the water suddenly go over your head! I'll do that by asking and answering four simple questions.

1. Why invest time in theological work in the first place? Aren't there better things for believers to be doing? Is our central task to try convincing critics about the correctness of our beliefs? Or should we concentrate instead on better understanding the faith for ourselves and actually living it rather than arguing about it?

2. Where should we start in our theology building--with a broad philosophic perspective or with our personal agendas, or immediate social circumstances, or what?

3. Should our goal be building a tightly reasoned system of thought or something more open and dynamic? How theoretical and systematic should—can— theology be? Is there hope that it can be practical and not just mind-stretching?

4. Is theology something that is delivered *to us* from the divine above or developed *by us* from our human below? Are we receiving it or creating it—or both?

5. My answer to most of these important questions is a simple "yes." We must be careful of the false simplicity of the either/or approach to things in the world of faith. Let's look more closely at these important opening questions. I will try to explain briefly my "yes" answer to each.

1. Why Do It? An important word in Christian theology is "apologetics." It doesn't mean we need to apologize to anyone about our faith, like we have done something wrong or believe something way off base. Rather, the idea comes from a Greek word that means "to give an answer or a defense." Do we want to respond to and even try to convince our critics? Sure. We have good news and should be anxious to share and do so as effectively as we can—although in the world of faith critics are seldom converted by mere argument.

And there are more than critics to be answered. There are natural disasters that raise difficult religious questions (volcanic eruptions, great floods, disastrous tornadoes, etc.). There is religious "pluralism," competing religious perspectives each claiming ultimate truth. There is moral "relativism," the claim that there is no ultimate truth, only individual perceptions related to given circumstances and people. And there are the natural sciences that occasionally claim that we can't believe anything if we cannot first find it physically and then measure and prove its reality and worth.

Weather disasters, deliberate genocide, other belief systems that claim ultimate truth, an anything-goes attitude in the general culture, specialists in this or that who discount the spiritual world altogether, these are very real challenges today and hardly to be ignored. Faith that has no legs on which to stand in the face of these kinds of things will surely fall—and probably deserves no better fate.

Serious believers in Jesus must engage in theological work if they are to grow in their understandings and be effective in their missions, but the work should never be done with a cocky attitude. Always remember that we are working in the faith arena. We would all agree if things were absolutely certain. So, faith is always needed. Stay humble even about your deepest convictions. Do know this for sure. The church needs good theology and so does the world in general. Note this bit of wisdom, which is also a warning:

> . . .contemporary theologians and ethicists write for other theologians and ethicists rather than for those in ministry. Which helps explain why those in ministry read fewer and fewer books on theology and ethics.... Theology, to be Christian, is by definition *practical*. Either it serves the formation of the church or it is trivial and inconsequential.[8]

Why engage in the work of theology? It's more than speaking to the critics and making sense of all the evil in this world. It also has to do with deepening one's own faith understanding and building up the church in the direction of all that she is called to be.

Doing theology well is crucial to the health and mission of the church. I engage in serious theological work—and hope you will--because I care deeply about "the formation of the church." Theology should help Christians be *more Christian*, more informed and more committed, more effective in spreading the good news.

Let me direct and plain. An uninformed faith that hardly goes beneath the surface of our thinking and living is almost as bad as none at all. If the church is not matured into being her true and vigorous and reflective self, her arguing with critics will be essentially a waste of time and her chances of making a real difference in this world will be few indeed.

2. Where should I start? One common choice about where to start your theological work is with a particular philosophy as your informing framework. Philosophies are systems of wisdom that try to orient our thinking about the really big issues of life. One system often tends to dominate a culture at a given time, and later gives way to another for a variety of reasons. Doing Christian theology happens within a particular context and cannot ignore the prevailing thought—likely it will interact with it, drawing ideas from it and refining it from distinctive Christian resources.

Should we start with the prevailing philosophy (there usually is one) and try to get a handle on Christian belief in light of it? Well, maybe not if we take our cue from Paul's failed attempt in Athens (Acts 17:16-34). Here was a city of idols and active Epicurean and Stoic philosophers ready to debate Paul. They did, Paul tried to adapt his message to their thinking by alluding to their "unknown god" and the writings of their poets, but it didn't go well. He decided it was better to stick to the central story of the Hebrew rendering of reality now fulfilled by Jesus and his dramatic resurrection from the dead. That rendering of things didn't fit well into the usual thought processes of Athens at the time.

Some of the earliest Christian theologians had more success in their attempts to integrate the good news of Jesus and given philosophic systems—at least temporarily and for particular audiences. Tertullian had a Stoic orientation and Origen a Platonic one (if you're not up on these names and philosophies, never mind for now). Tertullian's lawyer-like approach is echoed in many "conservative" circles today, while Origen's more academic approach is echoed in many "liberal" circles. The particulars come and go, but mind-sets and styles of approach seem rather standard.

In more recent generations, various prominent Christian theologians have begun with the philosophy Alfred North Whitehead and sought to build a "process" theology guided by his view of reality. Rudolf Bultmann began with "existentialism" and reinterpreted the teachings of the New Testament in its terms. Their work is valuable, although possibly not adequate and certainly not permanent representations of a sound theology that is distinctively Christian. The history of Christian theology is filled with experiments in cultural and philosophic adaptations. You will need to become acquainted with at least a few of these so that you can identify and critique your own. Let's leave that until later.

Social settings greatly influence the attitudes, language, and actions of the people living in them. Doing Christian theology inevitably interacts with the where/when of the theologian. After all, theology must make sense to the setting where it exists or it will not be understood, appreciated, or applied to life's needs. Even so, a given social setting likely is not the best place to begin.

Several recent theologians have produced "Liberation" or "Black" or "Womanist" theologies. They began with their strong concerns for the negative race, gender, or social injustice circumstances they faced and then moved on to restate the Christian tradition in ways that directly address their concerns. Their efforts have been insightful and valuable—and often controversial even among other Christian believers. None have come close to being the last word. Theological work is never done.

It's natural to begin theological work with yourself, what you know, and what you are experiencing, and there's a strong sense of relevance in doing things this way. The problem is that the result tends to be our immediate version of the faith and maybe not the historically-rooted and biblically-based faith itself. Good theology must express the faith in both *timeless* and *timely* ways. Accomplishing both is the really big job of any good theologian, and the job is never fully done.

We have seen too many Christians "strangle their evangelistic potential by barricading the ancient truths from an honest give-and-take with the realities of the moment. We also have seen too much of those Christians who are so anxious to be relevant that they parade curiously appealing 'theologies' that lack a direct tap root in ancient apostolic foundations of Christian faith.... Any serious statement of Christian theology must have some concern for the assumptions and requirements of the present cultural-intellectual situation, as well as some concern for the historic givens of Christian revelation."[9]

So, where do we start? First, begin with a sharp awareness of this double task—timeless and timely. Then embrace as a guiding principle that a truly *Christian* theology must be rooted in the biblical revelation of the reality and distinctive nature and purposes of God as known best in Jesus Christ That's an essential part of being "timeless." Be aware that there is variety of differing emphases even among Christians who accept this guiding principle. Here is a quick glance into this differing world—surely all that you are ready for at this point.

God is revealed biblically as "Triune," the great Three-in-One God. The classic Apostles' Creed has three central elements, Father, Son, and Spirit. The angle of our view and the emphasis of our thought make a real difference. To focus on the *Father* yields a creation or "natural" theology like those of Thomas Aquinas and modern theologians of ecology. To focus on the *Son* yields a redemption theology characteristic of Martin Luther and much of today's "evangelicalism." To focus on the Spirit yields an application theology common among "charismatics" and prominent theologians like John Wesley and Clark Pinnock.[10] Which is right? Again, the answer is "yes." Each is important, especially if not isolated from the wisdom of the others.

3. Where to head? I suggest that we theologians not try to compete with the philosophers by designing a new system of wisdom we think most appropriate for today's public, or by using an already-developed "secular" system of thought as the best way to rethink Christianity for our time. I intend to affirm that there is something distinctive about Christian faith that deserves to control the theological process, and that this faith is relevant in all times and places.

I further suggest that we not hope to construct a complex, tightly reasoned, and "systematic" theology that covers all the bases and answers all the questions. Some paradox, ambiguity, and mystery is inevitable—sorry! Any "god" we claim to understand fully is an idol of our own making. What we have in Christian faith is "less a cosmic Fact delivering to us a catalogue of facts about itself, and more of a Person, indeed, a heavenly Father who has come to us intimately...and calls for our faithful response as human persons to the divine Person.... Our human knowledge of this Father is real and adequate for our need. But it is so personal, so intimate, so enveloping of all meanings simultaneously that it is most appropriate to burst into song, rely on poetry, and resort to the use of parables. Jesus did, and he should be the center of our theology and the model of our practice.

Religious insight and experience move toward a depth and comprehensiveness that will not yield readily to "a captivity of simple sentences and terse definitions."[11] There's a special "grammar of grace" that is distinctive, and Christian theology must follow its unusual guidelines (see chapter 7). So, where should we head as beginning theologians? Not toward a finished system of thought that yields all the answers and is more sophisticated—and thus more right—than the thinking of the world around us. Know this. The Bible does gives less a finished system of theology and more a *compelling story* of God with us in Jesus Christ.

4. How to get there? Is Christian theology delivered to us or developed by us? Here it comes—the answer you might not like. The best and only adequate answer is "yes." If we do theology correctly, we will receive *and* refine. We will be instructed by divine grace, hear the great story, accept the God-offered relationship with Jesus, and then out of that relationship we will construct. It will proceed in light of our reason and experience, rooted in biblical revelation and assisted by the cumulative wisdom of the church's tradition of believing and teaching. We will honor divine revelation and then probe it with everything we are and have. That, of course, will require our identifying what really is from God, what it means, and how it can be stated clearly in the face of the accepted "wisdom" of our time.

Where do we go first? I suggest that we go back to Paul in Athens. He was anxious to share the message of Jesus with the diverse people around him. He and tried to accommodate his announcement of the message to the established assumptions of his hearers. He was heard as abrupt, outside the norm, and not worth hearing further. So he determined to go back to the basics—Jesus come from God and now resurrected from the dead. We seem to be left with two general options:

> **Optimistic Stance**: Authentic Christian faith centers in right relation to God and neighbors, with little necessary relationship to theological or philosophical speculation. Truth is subjectivity and there is a constant danger of over-theorizing it. People and relationships are the proper beginning points of theological reflection.

> **Pessimistic Stance**: Authentic Christian faith centers in receiving and being transformed by a divine revelation quite apart from ourselves. After all, we are "fallen" humans with impaired capacities for gaining truth on our own. Karl Barth, in the wake of the terrible World War I, released in 1919 his famous book *The Epistle to the Romans*. It was called a theological "bombshell" that declared the failure of the "liberal experiment." There must be a "wholly other" foundation to the faith, the Self-revelation of the Wholly-Other God.

Which is the best stance? One is more dynamic, relational, not necessarily aiming for intense thinking and formal statements of finished doctrine. The other leans more toward a distinctive revelation from God that trumps our "fallen" thinking and transcends our frail systems of belief and argument. So, which? Ready? The answer is "yes." Each is correct, at least to a point, although neither should ever be isolated from the other. There is a personal dimension to truth. Love of God and neighbor is essential. But we are fallen, sinful humans who hate as well as love. We must think hard about our faith, but always knowing that God's thoughts are always higher than ours.

Three pictures might help to sort out all of this. They are the focus of the next chapter.

4
HANGING THREE PICTURES

Question: What images should be in your head to get you off on the right theological foot?

Jesus was a master storyteller. He loved sharing parables as simple ways of conveying profound truths. He was a specialist in hanging word pictures in people's minds. He would ask stinging questions and answer set-up questions in ways that kept critical people off balance. Some loved it, others hated it, but most seemed to get his points.

I have three word-pictures in mind. They are mine, not exactly those of Jesus, but they represent well how he taught and are central to much of what he was teaching and living out and calling us to accept. They portray pitching a tent, singing a little song, and being entertained in an old barn. Ready for an interesting artistic ride? These pictures are keys to approaching Christian theology in the best ways.

PICTURES TO BE HUNG IN YOUR MIND

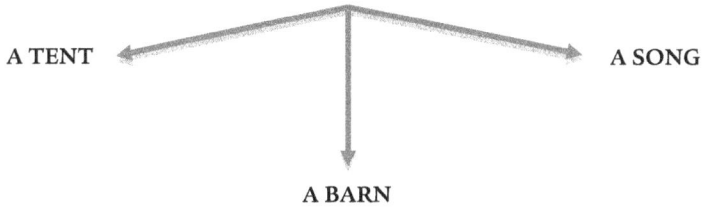

A TENT

A SONG

A BARN

The Tent Problem

Let's begin with the picture of a tent problem. Remember the English detective team of Sherlock Holmes and Dr. Watson? Never mind if you don't. Word has it that once they went on a fishing trip together. After a good meal and a soothing hot drink, they lay down for the night and went to sleep. Some hours later, Holmes nervously nudged awake his faithful friend Watson.

"Watson, look up at the sky and tell me what you see!"

Watson rubbed his eyes, looked up, and replied: "I see millions and millions of stars...What does that tell you?" asked Holmes.

Dr. Watson pondered for a minute, looked up more, and then in his overly academic way announced thoughtfully: "Astronomically, I see millions of galaxies and billions of planets. Astrologically, I observe that Saturn is in Leo. Horologically, I deduce that the time is approximately a quarter past three. Meterologically, I suspect that we will have a beautiful day tomorrow. Theologically, I can see that God is all powerful and that we are so insignificant.... By the way, what does it all tell you, Holmes?"

Holmes was quick to answer with a shocker completely unexpected: "Watson, you idiot. Somebody has stolen our tent!!"

There you are. Got the picture? In Christian theology, it's important to figure out which are the right questions and what are the real subjects. There are lots of distracting ghosts drifting about, distracting curiosities, files of irrelevant information, dead-ends of speculation. What should we be seeing and what is only distracting from what is right in front of us? Can we avoid getting lost in big words and cease being practical in the midst of layers of abstractions? Are we in danger of being so heavenly minded that we are of no earthly good? That seemed to be Watson's problem, and it has plagued many theologians. I want you to avoid spending much of your time on the wrong subjects, trying to answer questions of little or no importance.

On the other hand, there was Holmes with his own problem. We can be so concerned with the immediate and mundane that we fail to reach out in faith and see worlds and meanings well beyond the reach of the naked eye and the full comprehension of our little brains. Holmes was right, and so was Watson. And they both were a little wrong.

The Little Song

Are Christian theologians alien creatures? Let's leave the late-night tent theft and sample a simple song. A famous Christian theologian of a few years back once testified in a most interesting way. Karl Barth had authored his monumental *Church Dogmatics*, one of the most extensive and influential bodies of theological writing in all of Christian church history. Then came his final lecture in 1962. It was in the main auditorium of the University of Basel in Switzerland.

What should be the theme on this historic occasion? Probably an elaborate summary of his whole body of outstanding work, or maybe a sophisticated cap on all his celebrated sophistication. Would anyone not deep into theology books understand what Barth was about to say? Or does this truly wise man revert in humility to the most basic and plain with his concluding witness? The crowd sat in silence.

This aging and revered man rose slowly to his feet and announced that he would speak on love, *agape*, the perfect love of God that sovereignly seeks us humans, the very love of God so fully and wonderfully revealed in Jesus Christ. That was to be his surprisingly clear and simple theme—and yet, he said, maybe the most profound of all theological themes. His words were warm and clear. Barth appeared in a television interview shortly after and was asked what he knew for sure after all his thinking and writing and teaching over the decades. Again, surprisingly, he broke into the simplest of songs—"Jesus loves me, this I know, for the Bible tells me so."

Disarming. Wonderful. Demanding. Fundamental. The love of God in Jesus Christ is the highest reduced to the most basic. It was (is) vintage theology mined from the depths of searching and thinking that now was being reduced to the simple rhythms of a child's song. I have heard the Gospel of John described as so profound that the best thinkers will never plumb it all, and it also is so simple that the crowds heard and understood it quite well. Jesus asked the children to come to him. Are you interested in being a child? It's a great way to start being a theologian on the right track.

The Barn—Beware of the Exhaust!

Maybe city folks don't do well on rural camping trips. And when academic theologians appear in the world of ordinary Christians, the air can get a little chilly. Such an awkward scene of culture clash was once seen in Pennsylvania Amish country. A city family in their big car caught up to an Amish buggy being pulled by a tired-looking horse. There was a hand-printed sign on the back of the buggy—"Energy efficient vehicle. Runs on oats and grass. Caution—do not step in the exhaust!" What could that mean?

This culture clash is staged regularly in an old, red, and really round barn in northern Indiana. *Plain and Fancy* is a musical comedy from the 1950s with a serious storyline. You can identify with it if you've ever gotten lost on a lonely country road. If you are humble enough, you finally will stop and ask some farmer where you are. The city couple in this musical did stop once they were in full frustration. An old man with well-worn hands and a smiling face responded with classic words of direction.

"You are right here, of course, a really good place to be if you ask me!" That's nice, maybe right, but it doesn't help much. In the musical, directions are given to the lost and bewildered New Yorkers in a little song called "You Can't Miss It!" It is a tongue-in-cheek was of supposedly pointing the way to escape lostness. City folks just don't get the obvious.

Well, yes you can get lost in Amish country (or in Christian theology), unless you happen to know exactly where you're going in the first place and or set your GPS to be your guide—people in the 1950s would surely have wondered what those three letters were all about. Dan King and Ruth Winters didn't know about their destination, not exactly. They were trying to find Bird-in-Hand, an isolated place supposed to be somewhere in the Amish country of Lancaster County, Pennsylvania. Dan had inherited a farm there and wanted to see it and consider a neighboring Amish farmer's offer to buy. Getting there, however, was proving difficult for the "fancy" New Yorkers, alien creatures now traveling among the "plain" Amish—and I hope keeping a sharp eye out for any ugly carriage exhaust.

Got the picture? It can be just about like when traveling in the land of Christian theology. You can easily lose your way, even when an old-timer theologian tells you that the real truth just can't be missed. "Just read my books and copy my thoughts and conclusions and you'll have it." Really? Yes you can get lost, even when listening to someone who claims to have all of the answers. They tend to be the ones to be most careful of. The "plain" turns out to be "fancy," the straightforward can be as confusing as it is colorful. The way may be simple, but only if we can manage to find and claim it. Hearing again the echo of Barth's voice, whatever the simple turns out to be, in the land of Christian theology it will be in the territory of the loving grace of God.

Find and receive God's saving grace and you have found everything truly necessary. Don't overlook the missing tent—or the shining stars overhead without number. Pick up the complex score of a great symphony of God's creation—and sing the simple song of the love of Jesus. Christian theology is tough and tender, hard to find and always right in front of our noses.

We Must Keep Trying

To begin this treacherous but potentially joyous journey into Christian theology, let me admit that I have traveled this way before. I have tried to cover the territory, writing about Christian theology, but never as extensively or sophisticatedly as Karl Barth—although I hope I haven't missed his little song. About twenty years ago I wrote a "systematic" theology and called it *God As Loving Grace* (a little like Barth in focus and tone). Later I wrote *Radical Christianity*—was I getting a little extreme? At least I wasn't anywhere near being done.

Then came my book on God called *Discerning the Divine* (can we ever understand the One beyond our understanding?). And then there were other titles like *Caught Between Truths* and *The Heart of the Matter*.[12] It's plain enough that I'm really involved with this fancy theology thing and determined to find its heart, and now do so without dunking good ideas into thick mud so that you can't penetrate it with a sharp knife. I want to lead you to discover that the theological world can and should be, profound and life-changing, plain in its simplicity and relevant indeed to who you are, where you live, and ultimately where you'll be going later on.

In more recent years I have changed pace and wrote three novels. Jesus was something of a novelist, making up little stories to carry great truths. For me this change was a liberating experience, I confess. In the novel world you don't have to worry about the accuracy of every detail—after all, I was making up all the details from scratch. No more footnotes were needed. My sources were not from libraries and official-sounding online sites, but purely from somewhere in my head and heart. But even in my novels, spun from the world of my imagination, there were rules to be followed.

My wife, an English teacher, told me teasingly that in any good novel there has to be a plausible plot and a love story, even in a submarine at war with all men aboard. Not just anything could pass as acceptable. I hope I got things right in my *Coming Home*, *StarWalker*, and *In Deep Water* (about submarine warfare in World II and, yes, I got a woman on board in most unusual circumstances).[13] Is deep water where you are or fear you are about to be theologically? Try to relax. We will go slowly.

A plot must hold things together throughout a novel despite its various layers and unexpected twists and turns. Characters must be true to themselves in shifting circumstances. People need to know the past in order to understand the present. Context is important—you must make a reader feel that he or she is right there where the action is happening. Novels and theology have much in common.

The church needs to be aware of its current context. Relating to where it is means much to mission effectiveness. It also must learn from its own past contexts. After all, the good news the church hopes to share was formed long ago in languages and cultural contexts not familiar to most people these days. To not know these contexts of yesterday is to misread the good news that is to be shared today. Theology involves the deep plot behind the surface details of God with us, yesterday and today. It is the narrative that unveils the main character of the story, the God whose nature and purposes we must come to know from past revelation and then reflect in this world of our present mission.

Why write yet another book like this one? Did I fail to get the job done with all my other books? I hope not, and I still agree with what I once wrote. It's just that now I want to try lightening the mood, simplifying the language, and being sure that you, the reader, are never forgotten in a flood of difficult words that come easily in the theological world. I write here for you, the non-technical reader, not for my colleagues in the academic world. They have libraries of stuff already waiting to use up their time. I'm not needed there. It just may be that you need me now.

Don't misunderstand, please. I'm not assuming that you lack an adequate brain for heavy stuff. What I'm assuming is that you lack the needed background for doing theology, and if you did have the background you still wouldn't appreciate theology unless first you were convinced of its importance to your faith and life. What I write now must make sense and be relevant to who you are and where you are on your faith and life journeys. I will try not to disappoint.

I'm afraid. To borrow a few words from two special colleagues of mine: "We fear that Christianity may be in danger of becoming a mere 'folk religion,' relegated to realms of sheer subjectivity and emptied of public credibility.... We are also concerned that individual Christians who lack theological literacy and acumen will be tossed about by every wind of doctrine that comes sweeping through our media-dominated culture."[14] Put another way, doing theology with care will stop you from being satisfied with thoughtless emotion and being an easy target for the latest heretical scam.

I'm afraid for you and for me, and I'm hoping that I can help. Christianity is full of great feelings, but it's more than that. Its history is full of failures, but don't let that derail your journey. The church is more than its failures. Theology works with the *more* part, identifying what needs to be known and believed if religious feelings are not to be denied, church failures are not to be repeated, and the result is to be more than the false, empty, speculative, brainless, and self-serving "stuff" that fills the TV channels and social media outlets.

Here's a last thought for this chapter. Don't forget the tent, the song, and the barn. Each is an important signpost to not getting off track in theological studies.

5

LAND OF THE CORPSES

Questions: Can there be real life even in a cemetery?
 What should we do with what dies in church life?

In the lives of the church and the world, things come and go. Little stays the same for long. Likewise, ways of doing Christian theology remain in motion. Culture shifts, language changes, felt needs and social circumstances just won't hold still. The gospel of Jesus Christ doesn't change, but understanding it, expressing it in current language, and focusing its message to current needs are ongoing challenges.

One way to characterize the long and complex history of Christian theology isn't very pleasant. This history can be seen as a land of corpses, an antiquated array of now-failed attempts to express the faith in sets of fixed systems and doctrines and just don't work well anymore. However, and don't miss this, the impulse to keep at the theological task is persistent among Christians of all generations. Therefore, among the many corpses we see an ongoing parade of resurrections!

Maybe a little climatology could be pulled helpfully into the service of Christian theology. They say that the theological tradewinds blow from east to west. That means that particular theologies often have been created in Europe (especially Germany), have traveled to Scotland where they have gotten absorbed and powerfully preached, and then have drifted on westward clear to North America where they soon have been paraded and adapted, even perverted. By the time the "new world" gets into the act, something even newer already has been created back in the "old world" and is already starting west.

What can we learn from this pattern of theological climate moves? There will always be fads and fluctuations and personalities in the world of theology. The goal is more than getting on the latest theological bandwagon, although it may have something fresh and important to say. The goal is to get to the basics that are much more stable.

One of my mentors has been Helmut Thielicke—another European like Karl Barth. He has started some westward winds that still carry sustainable theological energy. I will let them pop up here and there in the rest of this chapter. As you pay attention and seek to find the mind of God for yourself and for this time in the church's history, keep an eye out for dead bodies, leftovers from now-exhausted theologies. Also stay open to new resurrections!

With all of this dying and rising, I want you to note carefully an important judgment that I agree with fully. "We do object to specific theologians and their ways of doing theology.... But we object just as strongly to any suggestion that theology itself—when rightly practiced—is spiritually deadening, unnecessarily divisive, merely speculative or ineffectual."[15] No generation of believers will get it just right, at least not just right for future generations living and serving in different circumstances. Even so, we are obligated to get it as right as possible for our own time and place. Theology may never be perfect, but neither is it ever optional.

Careful of the Bodies!

Let's get right to the persistent problem of theological corpses. You may need to hold your nose for this one. There have been monstrous wars fought over small points of theology and waves of emotion about a doctrine's exact wording. When you are sure that you are exactly right, and theologians sometimes think they are, even one inch of variance by a competitor can be judged intolerable and bodies could start falling. You could be the victimizer or the victim. The church can be a wonderful and a dangerous place for the simple and sincere soul, especially one with an independent mind.

A young Pakistani woman was shot in 2013 by the Islamic Taliban for advocating the education of females. Once safely away from Pakistan, recovering, and under the continuing threat of execution if she dared return home, she said this in an interview with the British Broadcasting Corporation: "Killing people, torturing people. . .it's totally against Islam. They are misusing the name of Islam."[16] Even if she's right, and I think and hope she is, the violence goes on, and unfortunately Jews and Christians have done the same over the centuries. Apparently, too much religion can be a dangerous thing. If the truth is totally plain to you, you may be tempted to think that dissenters deserve to be dealt with directly and decisively.

That young Pakistani woman's justified fear and impassioned plea for better understanding extends to Christian theology. Back to my mentor. Thielicke once reported the painfully obvious. Few congregations of Christians recognize or trust the worth of academic theology in church life. Often they actually fear it. Rarely has there been a theology student—myself included—who, reports Thielicke, "has not been earnestly and emphatically warned by some pious soul against the dubious undertaking of approaching Holy Scripture with scientific tools, against studying all 'doubtful questions,' and against casting himself into the arms of that omnivorous octopus, the unbelieving professor."[17] Careful who you hug, or who you let hug you, especially if they have academic letters after their names.

Who wants to be squeezed in the arms of a bunch of abstract ideas being delivered by a wayward professor who has lost his or her own way? For the young theologian—you, the simple fact is that spiritual growth must accompany intellectual expansion or one winds up suffocating in a library or at a computer screennwithout any divine oxygen to breathe. Complex ideas blow everywhere, but the life-giving wind of the Spirit of God can be rendered motionless in some dusty corner under a pile of books—some of which I may have written!

Don't misunderstand me. I am a big fan of libraries. Some years ago I oversaw the process of building an extension to a theological library. It was below ground and above it we built a beautiful new seminary chapel. We wanted seminary students to move freely from library and classrooms to the sanctuary of worship, from the books about life to the Spirit of life itself. Theological education is not an either-or business. Turn on your mind and keep your heart warm.

I'm sure that a few students over the years have seen me as that awful professor, if only because I encouraged the open consideration of all honest questions and options. I taught introduction to the Bible for many years on a conservative Christian campus. When I would mention some "prevailing scholarly viewpoint" on what Christian students just out of Sunday school considered a delicate and non-negotiable subject, one of them would smell an academic rat and see a heretic coming out of hiding.

What would such a student do when an unacceptable idea was considered in class? He or she would hurry to a phone after class (they didn't carry their own at the time) to alert a parent or pastor of the great danger the professor is to what was always taught at home. The concerned report is, "I think there might be heresy on campus and I'm having to pay for it!" After all, isn't thoughtful theology not much more than questioning God or challenging the authority of the Bible in favor of newer and very human ideas?

Let me ask you this. Can you imagine the God of the ages and of all spaces and peoples being floored by our choice to ignore and our refusal to obey? Who is God and how does God react to our many failures? Answering this question well lies at the heart of the Christian theological task.

I tried to be patient with students. After all, they were not used to thinking hard about faith issues, and certainly not hearing with tentative appreciation something put forward for consideration that disagreed with Grandma or a Sunday school teacher who had known everything about the Bible. Please remember that I don't know your grandmother personally and likely have never been to your Sunday school class, so don't take this as a slam on given individuals. What I'm downing is sometimes called "folk theology," unreflective believing, a mostly blind faith based on some tradition features this rigid motto, "This is how it is, period!"

Grandmas and Sunday school teachers are often little short of wonderful. I'm not criticizing the simple faith of uneducated saints of God. After all, I'm trying to be simple myself in these pages. What I'm criticizing is the wooden view that deep Christian spirituality and honest intellectual reflection are opposites and should not be allowed into the same room. I'm not much on bumper-sticker theologies that feature a quick emotion or outcome as the last word. Folk theology encourages gullibility and simplistic answers to difficult questions. Remember, I want for you the simple, but not the simplistic. We must try to keep in mind this crucial distinction.

The simple thrives on cute phrases and slick slogans. Stickers on the back of a car are hardly a good place for quality theology. They are easily misunderstood in the seconds people have to read and interpret them. My own mother had on her car bumper, "Have a Nice Forever." I assume she intended to encourage people by wishing that they might make it to heaven one day. But, in today's road-rage society, a quick glance at that could convey this message: "Give Me Room or Fall into the Big Fire!" Slogans mean what readers understand them to mean. We theologians must be careful with our words, which ones we use and where we decide to stick them.

Especially in the setting of "higher" education, we must not isolate ourselves from the world of competing ideas. That would be sheer arrogance and intellectual suicide. On the other hand (don't you hate these paradoxes?), we could lean on more words from my Dr. Thielicke. We Christians dare not be "victimized by the seduction of conceptual experience." What? He means that you should not allow yourself to be taken to the cleaners by fascinating new ideas that may be as groundless as they are tantalizing and temporary.

The grandmas of the world are not all wrong much of the time, not by any means—I had two grandpas who were right much of the time (just trying to keep my gender references balanced). How easy it is to be taken in by the new, the off-beat, the revolutionary theory. Our heads get caught up in the flash of advertising about the newest model and our feet hardly touch real ground. But isn't the newest always best? That's what advertisers are always saying. Some theologians often say this too, especially if very "liberal"; other theologians never do, especially if very "conservative." They are both on the edge of being wrong—and so am I, of course, by categorizing thinkers in this simplistic and highly suspect way.

Here comes Thielicke again. This one line of his has comforted--and humbled--me over the years, although it surely hasn't done either for all of my students. If a flashy new theological theory or style can be very wrong, it might also be right—at least for a given time and situation. There could be something new "under the sun" (as opposed to the pessimism of Ecclesiastes 1:9). Saying everything correctly (being "orthodox") can also be very wrong when spiritually lifeless inside. Said Thielicke: "Even an orthodox theologian can be spiritually dead, while perhaps a heretic crawls on forbidden bypaths to the sources of life."[18] What? Well, maybe.

Can you take that in? The same person can be fully right (orthodox), fully agreeing with traditional teaching, and yet be completely dead in terms of Spirit-life. Does right and dead equal wrong? Can the same person be all wrong (heretic) and still well on the way to finally being really right? Is what I'm saying wisdom or craziness? How do we know when we are being seduced by good-sounding new ideas? How can we tell which corpses are disgustingly *rotting* and which are wonderfully if not obviously *ripening*? Be warned, it's not easy to deal with all this theological stuff, even when we're putting it in plain language.

There's always a faith dimension to theology. If something is absolutely certain, there is no need for faith. Sometimes it comes down to how we are willing to look at things that are bigger than our little brains. I've heard that there are only two kinds of people in the world, those who wake up in the morning and gratefully say "Good morning, Lord" and the others who grump awake and mumble, "Good Lord, it's morning again!" In the first case, faith has kicked in and brought a warm glow to everything that remains darkness to others.

Theology: Common Objections

Know one thing for sure. We are *all* theologians if we are serious Christian believers and people of faith. We all should want to know better what we believe and try to find what that belief should mean for our living now and our situation hereafter, and also for the folks around us. Hear this well, please. You may be a *novice*-theologian, but you are not a *non*-theologian. Sorry about that if you don't want to be one. Theology is hardly an option—but *the kind you are* is an option, and a very important one. And since we all are theologians—or should be, let's work at becoming good ones. That's what the pages ahead are all about.

Know another thing for sure—something that is necessary for being a good theologian. It's about that "orthodox" (straight thinking) and yet that spiritually dead person mentioned above. I speak of the one who has it all right in traditional terms and still smells of serious wrongness, who has on ideal church clothes but has no real church on the inside. Hendrikus Berkhof, a famous Dutch theologian, once hit it right on the head. He envisioned an especially bad place in hell reserved for theologians more interested in their own theological thoughts than about God himself.

Here is an essential fact that perfumes the way to be a properly God-focused theologian. Have your brain open and active because you have *a heart for God*. Talking about God without knowing God personally is a dead-end game. If Berkhof is right, the dead-end will be especially hot!

The president of the university where I taught used to say, "when you're green you grow, when you're ripe you rot." He wanted us to stay open and keep learning—and that included the faculty who are already supposed to know a fair amount. But here's the subtle danger. Isn't green also the color of something going terribly wrong, like gangrene—the death of soft tissues? I want you and me to stay green only in the sense of being young at heart and on the growing edge in truth reception and understanding. I have been called a theologian who is on the progressive (green) side of the middle. I like that designation. One tends to rot when at either extreme that is too far away from the middle.

So here we are. Let's risk being green, all of us theological novices who are willing to listen, test, think, and grow. Never close your eyes to what is definitely rotting (although you may pinch you nose to avoid gagging). But also never be too quick to judge what is really happening. Green is sometimes good--and sometimes very bad.

My European mentor—you know his name by now--speaks of "theological puberty." He warns that we shouldn't try singing solos when our voices are changing. Nor should we try expounding intellectual insights about Christian theology until our internal spiritual organs and our theological brain cells have both matured enough to warrant going it alone and out-loud. Learn before you teach.

If you are patient, puberty eventually passes. Hang in here with me! Without being filled by the love and wisdom of God, which Karl Barth was talking about and which doesn't happen overnight, a theologian can begin to smell like the corpse of lifeless ideas. On the other hand, never forget what Helmut Thielicke said. A true searcher after truth can "crawl on forbidden bypaths to the sources of life." I really want us to crawl in the right direction—and without smelling up the place!

Many voices caution against getting involved with theology. Two of my theological friends (both non-Europeans this time) have summarized the standard objections. They are heard all the time. Each objection has a point—it's just not as sharp as it seems when pointed right at you. My friends call the objections Killjoy, Divisive, Speculative, and Stalemate. They're pretty obvious. You might be tempted to avoid theology because of by any or all of them.

- Theology can be abstract and take all the life and fun out of religion.
  I don't want you to merely to sit up straight and recite cold creeds.

- Theology can inspire the formation of tribes of believers (denominations) that become painfully ingrown and competitive. Jesus unites, say the objectors, but theology divides.
    I don't want you to be identifying the winners and losers so that you can stay in charge.
- Theology can lose us poor believers in intense efforts at trying to find out what can't be found out, wasting time delving into mysteries beyond the range of possible human understanding.
    I certainly don't want you to engage in speculation that only wastes time.
- Theology can work hard and get mostly nowhere—as it has for centuries, coming up with fresh solutions to old dilemmas that only give the next group of theologians something to work on and revise again.
    I want us to get somewhere, not going in the perennial circles of yesterday's intellects. But neither do I not want you to assume that all of that past work (tradition) was useless.

Please don't misunderstand. I'm not suggesting that these oft-heard objections have the last word. Still, they have lots of words that cannot be ignored easily. You may be quite impressed with one or more of them. Be patient. The whole story has not yet been told.

Sacred or Diabolical?

Now let's get back to the positive. We can stiffen in the freezer of theology or be warmed by its being done well and emerge into the richness of life that is truly alive in the highest possible sense. Look out—here comes Thielicke again. What can and should good Christian theology do for us and the church? Having glanced at the standard objections, good theology nonetheless can and should be

> ...the conscience of the congregation of Christ, its compass and with it all a praise-song of ideas.... Theology is a very human business, a craft, and sometimes an art. In the last analysis it is always ambivalent. It can be sacred theology or diabolical theology. That depends upon the hands and hearts which further it.[19]

I vote for the sacred. We must care for our hands and our hearts, and also our heads. Theology lies somewhere between being a human craft and a divine art.

What are the possible benefits of doing theology well? We should wind up respecting and loving each other. We should be assured that we have not been wasting time on the impossible, and we should be having fun in the process, bringing praise to God and joy to ourselves and our neighbors.

Ambivalent about your readiness to do this well? That's natural. My mentor says that a little of that hesitancy will always remain. We will never have all the answers or the last word. I am still only human. How about you? Let's see if we can manage something good together, gaining significant if not ultimate understanding of God and God's ways with us. Theology is pursuing an important first stage of understanding, if not the finished product.

Never forget that there are corpses to look out for and objections that won't go away just because we begin to make good progress. There also, however, is the great potential of "a praise-song of ideas." Theological study can be a danger to the faith. So can overeating and overworking. Is the answer to quit studying and eating and working altogether? Hardly. The antidote for bad theology is not *no* theology. It is *good* theology! Much of our task from here on is trying to figure out what makes up the "good" of the theology that our hearts and congregations and communities today need so badly.

Our task is not easy and you may get wide-eyed at the fact that there is a *deadly duo* that I am about to choose and follow on the way to the good. Hang on while I explain what that is and why it is necessary. Our good-theology road has deep ditches along its sides and a big hole or two right in the middle. No matter. We can make it with tires and mufflers in tact. After all, we are about God's business as we seek to think God's thoughts and then live godly lives.

6

A DEADLY DUO
(or a Perfect Pair?)

Questions: Are you willing to go beyond the beating heart to the thinking brain? Do you dislike grammar, preferring the emotional highs of unleashed disorder?

When I was younger I sometimes was privileged to hear a father and son sing together before large church gatherings. Dale and Doug Oldham were showstoppers! Other duos, however, are more likely to be show-slammers. So, an immediate admission is in order.

I might be shooting myself in the foot in how I am about to explain the proper doing of Christian theology. I am going to encourage an embracing of what sounds like a deadly duo. Why two, and why choose what it likely deadly to your continuing interest in the subject? Answering will take a little time, but I am sticking with my duo, hoping that it will not be deadly after all.

How Dumb Are You?

I read a little book a few years ago that critiqued much of contemporary theology. It reported that so many theologians write for each other, sometimes to gain higher status in a university professorship, that they leave the typical preacher and certainly the average believer in the academic dust. Are theologians trying to convince non-academics "that they are too dumb to understand real theology,"[20] or are they just not that interested in the lives of local churches and everyday believers?

Maybe that's why so many ministers are not reading many theology books these days. The content is far from useable in the pulpit or the pew. But this is all wrong. Christian theology is to be practical, serving the formation of the people into Christ's image so that they can think and love and serve like Jesus today. Otherwise, theology is trivial, inconsequential, the enterprise of the church's elite that is hardly understandable by the rank and file of believers.

Is this your attitude? "Give me Jesus--and then let me alone!" Well, if you've really got Jesus (or better, if he's really got you), remember that he let very little alone—including his slow-to-learn and often confused disciples. He reinterpreted his Jewish tradition, challenged wayward religious practices, built a community of believers around a new vision of faith, and stayed in close touch with his Father as he upset establishments and introduced a new age for all humanity. That's a lot of not letting alone! Figuring out who this Jesus was—and is—and knowing how to think and act like him will take some considerable brain and heart stretching (key theological exercises). Being true to Jesus is being willing to be stretched.

Jesus asks his disciples to come and follow him, to figure him out and become like him. As Thielicke says, theology can be the conscience and compass, the sacred art form desperately needed by the church. A faithful following of Jesus can lead to some wonderful places. So, am I complicating the Christian life unnecessarily by insisting on doing the theology thing or am I just repeating what Jesus said and did and expects? Here's where the *deadly duo* comes in. I'm going to write about Christian theology from the point of view of *grammar*, the subject many high school students say they like least of all. Are you ready for both theology and grammar? What more can I say to drive you to some detective novel or smart-phone game or television sit-com? Theology and grammar--a deadly duo to be sure!

Let me offer some basic definitions so that you will know better what I'm talking about. I will offer the simplest ones possible, at least to get started.

Theology—faith in God that is seeking more understanding of God. It is believers searching for how best to gain and express God-centered beliefs and live a God-centered existence informed and inspired by Jesus Christ—who is the central theological subject.

Grammar—the groundwork or roadmap for how the words we use can form clear and attractive sentences for carrying our thinking and believing and speaking about God. We are searching for the best way for our words to relate to each other so that the result is excellent and even colorful communication that attracts others to Christ.

The Deadly Duo—a merging of the searching of theology and the grace-filled rules of divine grammar, two underappreciated enterprises that need each other. They are vital for any Christian seeking the best way to understand and express in wise and living sentences the meaning of Christian faith for today's personal and public lives. I insist that this deadly duo is actually *the perfect pair*. We must gain proper understandings and discover potent ways of wording and sharing them.

We must come to know the true identity of Jesus who is the proper subject of every Christian theological sentence. And we must be filled by Christ's Spirit who is the necessary verb of true Christian understanding and all true Christian living. The Spirit inspires a deep understanding of the Jesus-truth and empowers all adequate living out of Christ's way of life.

Do such definitions clarify things for you? I hope so. Either way, here I am, in what might be the worst of all positions to gain your favor. I want you to increasingly appreciate the importance of the perfect pair, and I'll do all I can to help you get there.

I just heard a wonderful sermon emphasizing what Jesus told his disciples before he left them to return to his Father. He promised the sending of his Spirit who would interpret and activate in his disciples all that he had been and said and done (John 15:14-17, 16:12-15). The preacher said so rightly that "Jesus is the *subject* and his Spirit is the *verb*. That's basic. One without the other is little or nothing. Together they form the most lovely sentence of all—*Jesus is still alive and now is alive in me!*

Never doubt that little grammatical things can make a lot of difference. Speech patterns can be confusing and inconsistent—especially in English. If it is *he*, *his*, and *him*, is there any rational reason why it also should not be *she*, *shis*, and *shim*? I'm not sure about the reason, but it just isn't that way. Beyond the inconsistencies, missing bits of language parts make big differences in the meaning conveyed. Punctuation marks help or hinder greatly the actual meaning of even properly ordered and related words.

On a recent road trip I saw three commercial signs grabbing for my attention. I wish I hadn't paid attention because they carried errors, very little ones that made the messages all wrong—I wonder if someone got fired because of these foiled messages? Might disciples of Jesus be dumped from the list of the holy ones because they persist in sending the wrong messages to the world by their sloppy and inattentive theological constructs and life languages? Whatever the answer, here are the mixed-up road signs I saw.

High over a motel stood a giant sign blazing its message down on the interstate. Ready for this? "Best Rats in Town." Might an "e" in the second word have helped? Personally, I prefer sleeping with blankets and not rodents, however cheap the charge for the room.

Another sign had all the words spelled right. It's just that there were no punctuation marks where they would have helped. It was in front of a grimy gas station and said this: "Jesus Saves Old Batteries and Tires." Since there was no comma after "Saves," naturally I wondered why Jesus did such an odd thing. What exactly does Jesus save, and why? I wonder where he keeps all of his old car parts. Does he recycle? I've often seen the sign "Jesus Saves." The modern reader is left to guess from what—apparently not traffic jams.

And then there was this sign hanging over a fast-food place: "Breakfast biscuit with cheese only $333." Without a decimal point in a strategic place, that bite of breakfast had gotten very expensive! Only one letter missing, one comma not there, one period forgotten, but what a difference such things make! Theology is both the substance of what we believe and the sentences by which we try to frame and share it. We must be careful of our spelling, punctuating, and decimal placing.

Let me stretch your patience further as I try to continue explaining myself. Before us is a deadly duo, actually the perfect pair of theology framed by God's grammar. We are approaching Christian theology with grammar in mind as a crucial vehicle for understanding and communicating. As I write these lines, I am in a restaurant and it's noisy in the next booth. This awkward setting holds another important theological lesson.

A group of Hispanic workmen are relaxing over lunch and speaking their Spanish very rapidly. They are gushing flurries of words with perfect understanding—theirs, not mine. I know that it may be just as hard for you to make sense of a lot of theology talk. You could always move to another booth, or learn the talk, or I could slow down the flow of strange words and use only ones your ears are ready to handle. That third option is what I'll try to do in the pages to come. So, on I go, assuming the wisdom of taking with me into the world of Christian theology the essential guides, the deadly duo, the perfect pair.

Beyond Warm Fuzzies

Be aware that in nothing that follows am I meaning to debunk all rules of conduct or systems of thought—or your grandmother's folk wisdom about all things mundane and divine. I am a theologian after all, and I don't even know your grandmother! I am only cautioning about the danger of excess in these directions, and I'm trying to keep the language under control—while still insisting that careful use of language is of great importance. With all this in mind, I do hope you take the following paragraph *personally*.

You may be a Christian who wants good religious feelings, not theological words to figure out and religious rules to follow. That's great, but only to a point. We humans are made to feel deeply, and part of how we come to know involves how we come to feel. But too much reliance on feelings is a dangerous business, a sure path to theology going off track.

If you insist that your only goal as a believer is experiencing great religious feelings, apart from careful theological thought, I say this to you. Enjoy your shallow self as you are bounced about by every wind of doctrine and wave of emotion that blows and flows your way. Go ahead and risk believing what could be no more than your personal prejudices parading as pleasant biblical teachings. Go ahead and be a believing body that is alive but risks any ability to function in our world of competing beliefs because your arms and legs are nothing but soft tissue without any bones. Go ahead. Just sing your little songs, do your little dances, and leave your faith at that. Be a folk theologian with your head in the blinding sand—let's not think what might be happening to the rest of you! That's your choice, faulty as it may be.

Whatever you do or don't do, some kind of theology will find its way in. Would you prefer to be an accidental or intentional theologian? There are particular views you hold about your faith whether you know it or not. An unexamined faith can be faulty, or worse, and you not know the difference. You need to be in touch with your views and values, and maybe even move beyond some of them. Do you know what they are? Do they lack a carefully considered logic that squares with the thought patterns of the Bible? Are you a pleasant but immature religious blob who is having a good time in church even though your skeleton-less spiritual life can't stand or walk and resists thinking about itself critically? I apologize if that question seems too harsh.

Are you just uninterested in going on from the beating heart to the thinking brain? That might make you happy, but I'm telling you that it saddens the God who wants you to be an adult believer and a credible witness in this world. And it makes the enemy of your faith smile. You are a babe in the woods, an easy target, a grammatical mess, a source of convoluted communications, a happy child wandering innocently in a jungle of ideas anxious to devour.

The stakes are so high for the mission of the Christian community. I know that becoming all brain and no heart would be just as bad as being only a brainless glob of warm fuzzies. We're all hunting for the right balance. Please keep hunting with me.

A Strange Land

Let me tell you how I got started on this present foray into a lighter style of theological writing. My wife and I were in Iceland, that fascinating land of fire and ice, volcanoes and moonscapes. At some point in our visit I realized that this big island, kind of a world of its own in the North Atlantic, is much like Christian theology in several ways.

The island is confusing right off. Neighboring Greenland has much of the ice and Iceland most of the green. Oh well. Iceland is a place off the beaten track of the usual shipping lanes, and certainly it isn't the typical tourist attraction. It's an ancient place, and yet parts of it change every day and keep being brand new. The primary energy source on the island comes from deep in the Earth, geothermal they call it. Large stretches of the island's surface are unusual indeed, flat lava fields hardly passable on foot and almost beyond description. When you see them, you tend to just stare to be sure it's all real. Sound a little like theology?

Scientists are good at technical descriptions of Iceland, and they are convinced that attempts at understanding this old place are very important. The island tells us many things about the past of our planet—and maybe its future. Someone on our touring bus said, "What happens in Iceland does not stay in Iceland. It's as bad as losing control of yourself in Las Vegas. What happens, good or bad, finally gets out and can affect negatively your whole world. For example, a few years ago one of Iceland's volcanic eruptions shut down for days all air travel in Western Europe. What happens to the ice in that area of the world can change the level of the oceans of the whole planet. Not a small thing, and it is happening! Can you swim?

Alright, enough of history, geology, and scare tactics. Let's travel. We are now heading for Iceland, and for the strange world of Christian theology. I'm your guide. I'll stay with the English language (no heavy theology speak). Icelandic is an odd-sounding language to the untrained ear. The Vikings can have it. Maybe that's why they sailed away from this Iceland homeland of theirs so often and strayed so far away. Maybe.

Word is that the Vikings made it clear to North America long before Mr. Columbus came there from Europe. Apparently the exploring Icelanders didn't stay long because the natives of today's Canada were just too troublesome and the hassle not worth the costs of colonizing. The later Europeans obviously disagreed. If the Vikings had stayed, maybe today we would all be wearing funny hats, going to school in longboats, and vacationing by going back to mother Iceland.

Is that how you're feeling right now about Christian theology? Is it too far away and not worth the hassle, too strange a language and too disconnected from your daily to-do list? If so, don't let it get to you. You're not the first, and you must allow for the possibility that feelings are often out of touch with what is really real and possible and worthwhile.

With my help I hope your little trip into theological Icelandic, even if a bit of a hassle, turns out to be worth it. Forget the old Vikings and please stay for a while. They're all dead and their meager leftovers are mostly in museums. By contrast, good theology, while ancient in its roots, can be richly relevant to every today.

7

GOD'S GRACE GRAMMAR

Questions: Would you have removed grammar from your school curriculum? Did you know that God has a special grammar that is truly divine?

Here we go on our theological journey! We will be making a comfort stop occasionally, so try to relax and open your mind. As you do, remain aware that the use of your mind will have its important roles and its definite limitations. Reason and logic, although critical for our theological task, are rarely the only or even the last word. Things in this world are dependable, unless they aren't. Faith values reason but also goes beyond its limited reach. It comes to know the truth of this classic statement:

> The real trouble with this world of ours is not that it is an unreasonable world, nor even that it is a reasonable one. The commonest kind of trouble is that it is nearly reasonable, but not quite. Life is not an illogicality; yet it is a trap for logicians.[21]

What Did You Say?

Let's start with the obvious. Things in this world seem to change so much, even while other things are always the same. Your smart phone or laptop is outdated before you can learn how to use it. Capitalism is an economic system based on the encouragement of constant selling and buying. "Be a good citizen," it calls to you, "and never be satisfied with what you now have. Always rush out and get the newest of whatever." On the other hand, the federal government seems most worthy of our criticism—we can always count on that! Then there's the church. Again, if you have a mind to, there's always something to complain about.

Theological work has to lean on language and honor the rules of a distinct grammar to make its unique sense and be true to biblical revelation. So, to be good theologians, we must face the fact that using language well faces the challenge of the constant change of language itself. Here's a simple example of shifting language. This is treacherous territory, so be careful. Words won't hold still even when you're trying to use them properly for Christian purposes.

For many years my wife, a retired high-school English teacher, would make her students memorize and then recite a portion of the famous *Canterbury Tales* in its original middle-English form that dates back to the late fourteenth century. Oh how they complained! It was a great mental exercise, one that most "modern" kids, at least at first, think is exceptionally hard, even stupid. Then there's the King James translation of the Bible that dates back to 1611. The English spoken in that time of England's history sounds today like semi-riddles that can bring confused smiles--if it's understood at all.

Some older folks in our churches, especially if coming from very conservative and traditional families and Sunday schools, memorized Bible verses in their childhoods from the King James translation. They still are convinced that this version somehow has the special stamp of God on it—despite the rather crass political situation that spawned its beginning, the relatively inadequate biblical source documents it had to work with, and its verbal cadence that is marching to some English king not particularly respectable and long dead. To their ears the quaint language style still has a heavenly ring to it.

So be it. That's perfectly understandable. Classic verses like John 3:16 rendered in the old version still work well for most of us, but many verses do not. Here is a verse from the Song of Solomon in the King James version. It is spoken by a lover whose beloved has just arrived: "My beloved put in his hand by the hole of the door, and my bowels were moved for him." Sound romantic to you? We now tend to think of the seat of our emotions as the "heart." Obviously there was a time when the seat was much lower down. Be careful how you say what you say.

Using words correctly involves good timing and proper nuance that fits the immediate context and the ears of the hearers. That's why this present book is trying to look at Christian theology in the language of life today, language that makes sense to most modern ears. Language is an art form always in motion. Grammar is an essential part of good language—sorry. It's more than boring rules of how to write and speak properly. It's about what makes up clear thinking and effective communication; it's about finding the right words and using them rightly so that they relate well to their surroundings. Since we believers are on mission for Jesus, we must relate well to those who need him.

A good friend of mine is really sensitive about this subject and wrote his book *Masterful Living* precisely because word meanings had changed in relation to Christian "holiness." Kevin Mannoia hoped to introduce a new vocabulary that could freshly express old theological truths.[22] Hubert Harriman and I did the same thing in our book *Color Me Holy!* and I did again in my *Catch Your Breath!* Now I'm trying to encourage you to think about the task of fresh theological expression in relation to the whole range of Christian teachings. Thinking well and turning your thought into effective communication requires a skilled use of grammar that is both human and divine (I'll explain the divine part momentarily).

Do you understand how important language is to Christian theology? A vibrant vocabulary is necessary. Living doctrines need to be dressed in proper language clothes and stated with the grammatical grace they deserve—otherwise they will convey wrong messages. They must be designed to speak clearly to the people within range of your voice or the reach of your smart phone or electronic tablet (that's about everybody these days). We want a contemporary way of talking that doesn't sound like a ramped-up rapper who talks so fast and spits out such strange images that you know he must be high on something other than clear communication. Added to the choice of good words must be a good grammar. By that I mean gaining the skill necessary to deploy well the good words we find to use. I also mean coming to realize that human language, when used in the service of Christian theology, must yield to a special set of divine guidelines (grammar) that flavors it all in a unique way.

Christian theology relies on a careful use of words chosen with sensitivity to the listening audience. But I want to convince you that something else is necessary. Theology also involves a special standard and guide that should control how we pick and put together our words—a special grammar, God's *grace grammar*. This pattern of choosing and relating words to form belief statements is distinctive to Christian revelation. The traditional claim is that it is of divine origin (revealed and inspired) and brings marvelous meanings beyond normal abilities or human experiences.

To make sense of this will take lots of words of mine. I hope I find the right ones for you, ones that will penetrate both your brain and heart and stay true to God's distinctive speaking to us humans. It has been said that theology is a careful thinking of God's thoughts after him. We are cautioned, however: "So also no one comprehends what is truly God's except the Spirit of God" (1 Cor. 2:11). Apparently our thinking God's thoughts can only be done as a gift of God's Spirit. The proper grammar of Christian theology always is a grace gift.

More Alive Than Religious

There is, for the Christian at least, a pattern of meanings and a manner of expressing them that I am calling the grammar of divine grace. As an advance hint of what this means, we might say this. Christian theology explores how God's grace-grammar transcends the normal logic of human language, how it brings a new, a less-structured, even a wordless kind of thinking and speaking. One writer has tried to put this beyond-words thing into words (oh my!):

> When human beings enter into the joyful celebration of the glory of God and the goodness of God's gift of life [grace], normal prose breaks into poetry, normal voices break into song, normal postures break into dancing [a special grammar], and people don't simply become more *religious*—they become more *alive*.[23]

What do you think of that? It is better to be really alive, spiritually alive, than to be really religious? Maybe being really alive is the best way to be truly religious. Where does this aliveness come from and how do we think about, put it into effective words, and spread its good news? These are basic questions. Christian theology is about finding, expressing, and implementing good answers to them.

What's the best description of what Jesus was doing when physically on this earth? Was he trying to start a new religion, get rid of his own too-old and law-strangled Judaism? Hardly. He wasn't anxious to "start a new religious argument about dogma-mountains; it was to fill hearts with Spiritfountains. . .to help everyone become like little children through Spirit-birth."[24] He was Life bringing life.

There are key elements of the theological agenda. Good theology, beyond belief foundations, will highlight the dynamic realities of the presence and grace-full work of God's Spirit that enables new life.

Listen to Jesus: "He called a child, whom he put among them, and said, 'Truly I tell you, unless you change and become like children, you will never enter the kingdom of heaven'" (Matt. 18:2-3). Here's the way, the Jesus way. It is the way of being simple without being anywhere close to simplistic. Here's great wisdom that recognizes and accepts the humility and joy and innocence of a child. Here's a grammar of pure and wonderful grace, God's way of structuring the sentences of our redeemed and reborn lives. The result is a special kind of communication, proper theology-talk bathed in and lived by God's grace. Its purpose is new life and not just more talk or proper practice.

This grammar of grace, this beyond-words best way to use words, erupts from God's undeserved grace showered our way. If this grace is gratefully received, it tends to flow through us, inspiring a particular way of thinking, believing, talking, and acting. It comes from the deepest of all things, God, and speaks to wherever is deepest in us. Paul gloried in being "fools" for Christ because God's wisdom is higher than any that comes from humans (1 Cor. 3:19). As we bow low we find ourselves in the heights of God's truth and new life.

All of the cross-of-Jesus business is "foolishness to those who are perishing, but to us who are being saved it is the power of God" (1 Cor. 1:18). What do we see when looking at a page of print? The same words can be read to mean very different things. In part, the ministry of God's Spirit is that of a reading teacher. We are helped to become literate in the things of God. How does this happen? It happens by our becoming newly alive by the grace of God mediated through the Spirit. This life sharpens our reading skill, our understanding of God and God's truth.

Real people like Saul (Paul) had experienced a change of life channels and had come to follow a different plot line for living. They had gotten caught up in a different story of what is really real. History had become for them *History*, a divine drama being played out and revealed from above and within. Old words had come to have new meanings because early Christians had become freshly related to each other by a new grammar that is loaded with life-changing grace.

Back to Iceland. This new grace grammar of God is the geothermal power and energy coming from a distant place usually inaccessible to us—thus the need for God to "reveal" it, bring it, let it happen for us. God's grace-full grammar is a sustainable energy source that can warm our bodies and homes and communities when the harsh winters come. It can fire imaginations outside our usual boxes. It is the carrier of divine vision, the illuminator of divine truth.

Let's put this grace-energy back to the first-century Roman world. God's geothermal grammar helped a crazy crew of Jesus' disciples turn the world upside down with some really strange good news. It was especially good if you could actually understand and believe it. Could a failed and humiliated prophet from Nazareth (where is that?) really be the wave of the whole world's future? Could a crucified Christ be carrying the power of the Creator when he seemed unable to avoid his own execution? That surely sounds like garbled grammar, nonsense sentences.

To the general public of the time, the answers were obvious negatives. It was nonsense. That's still the case. But to Paul there was a determination to know only Christ and his resurrection, even if all of Athens could not read the seemingly silly sentence that way (Acts 17). Can you roll with that? To use a common image today, can you honestly put your hands together and "give it up" for a humiliated Nazarene of centuries long gone who claimed to be the presence of the future? The future comes when you can, and it fades when you can't.

This grace grammar, this reverse reading of reality, was set up by Jesus as a divine gift of life that mere words cannot capture, although we must try to use well the words we have (that use is doing theology). Check out these inspired lines:

> More tender than we can imagine,
> More faithful than we can conceive,
> Stronger than we can envision,
> Wiser than we can believe—
>
> What loss through our blindness we suffer
> When God's boundless love we ignore;
> But when we just taste of its sweetness,
> 'Tis then we fall down and adore![25]

This is a little of the "breaking into poetry" mentioned above. It's the high-end grammar of God's amazing grace. There is sight beyond our seeing. There is rationality beyond our reasoning. We should stand up and face this, fall down and accept it, and just adore. Taking a bite of this unparalleled sweetness begins to enable—demand—a new language of life, a theology revealed by God.

There is something in the larger reality of creation that is beyond our imagination and wisdom. The good news is that, although beyond us, it has been offered to us undeservedly for our tasting and sharing. If we will just bend down in humility, we will wind up standing taller than ever. We grow upward precisely because we are willing to fall downward. Isn't that a strange grammar, a reverse logic, a weird combination of concepts? It's like Jesus himself. Either he was all the amazing things he said about himself or he was truly deluded and should have been locked up long before he was executed! His resurrection convinced his first disciples that *amazing* is the normal adjective for Jesus—and the hope for us!

A Reliable Foundation

One of the first books I encountered as a new seminarian had been written by the imposing man about to teach me New Testament Greek. His book's premise caught me off guard. I had come to seminary to learn to be a Christian minister, not to extend my college English major. But this professor and his book led me right back to the critical importance of the structure of language for expressing proper Christian believing. Listen to this from his book (and don't be distracted by the male language—he wrote it in 1958): "A person cannot be a theologian unless he is first a grammarian.... He who knows best what the vocabulary of Scripture meant to the writers who used it can best gain access to the message which those writers sought to convey. The devices and idioms of speech are of tremendous importance. Consequently, grammatical study is a responsibility of the first magnitude for man in his search for the truths of life and destiny."[26]

Here's the good news—and I'm assuming that you are not a big fan of the details of the grammar of language. While my old prof goes into great detail about the various parts of speech and the nuances of their many meanings, I am going to stick mostly to the *central nouns and verbs* critical to understanding and living the Christian faith. I will roam a little farther afield in a later chapter on "bench players." Don't ever think that adverbs, adjectives, and punctuation marks are of little importance. They can change the meaning of a sentence dramatically. I'm trying to present theology in plain language not bound up in layers of complex grammar and unfamiliar vocabulary.

Christian theology needs a vibrant vocabulary that communicates well in part by using the right grammar to deploy the words in proper relation to each other. Can you hang with me while we try unfolding of some of this? God has been especially good to us messed-up humans. We surely haven't deserved it. That's *grace*. The overflow of the meanings and implications of how this grace works in highly unusual ways is a distinctive *grammar*. Tracking these ways in an ordered fashion is *doing theology*, following the pathways of God's grace as they play out in our own words and world.

8
BACK TO THE BASICS

Question: Theology rarely comes in complete sentences. Can you live with not having the last word in theological matters?

In the pages to come we will explore this special God-grammar for understanding what Christian belief and life are all about. It is a grammar that follows the unusual rules established by the particular patterns of divine grace known most fully in Jesus Christ. It's a wonderland that puts Disney on the sidelines. The all-powerful God of the universe is known best, so this biblical story goes, in a helpless baby born in an isolated Palestinian barn.

The Gospel in a Nutshell

Here's a quick summary of this strange way of finding and putting together the biggest truths of all. God *is*; God is *good*; God in his goodness has wanted us *to know* about all this so there could be dissolved the tragic gulf between us and God. So God provided all that was needed—*himself in flesh* (Jesus). There it is, everything in four simple points. John's Gospel begins with a report of this dramatic divine communication. "In the beginning was the Word, and the Word was with God, and the Word was God.... He came to what was his own..." (Jn. 1:1, 11). Plain enough? God is. God loves. God acts to redeem. God comes, personally, and his name was Jesus.

Here is the really big theological sentence—not long, just big. "God has spoken in Jesus!" The eternal word was verbalized clearly in one man, a real man in whom we language-starved humans can see, hear, and understand. Later in the New Testament we read: "We declare to you what was from the beginning, what we have heard, what we have seen with our eyes, what we have looked at and touched with our hands, concerning the word of life..." (1 Jn. 1:1). And there is more. This Jesus now has sent his Spirit to keep us in touch and to activate in and through us the redemptive benefits and mission gifts that we so much need. Quite a story!

Where do we get this stunning information? The Bible is the basic source of divine revelation. What we have comes from God as known in Jesus Christ (he is *the* revelation). It now comes to us primarily through the book that conveys Christ to us with the help of Christ's interpreting Spirit. One little boy announced to his father what he had heard somewhere about what the Bible really is. It stands, he said, for "Basic Information Before Leaving Earth!" Out of the mouths of babes.

There it is, the Christian gospel in a nutshell. It's primarily about Jesus, put in the words of a book, with all of it coming to us by an undeserved divine grace through the Spirit. That grace has been spoken into where we live in words that we actually can get, in sentences that the Spirit helps us read. And theology? Christian theology is the careful process of following the meanings of that Word (Jesus) in the biblical words and bringing them into fresh words that can penetrate every corner of our believing, theologizing, and living.

God's being and undeserved but shared goodness (grace) is the base, the grand subject. Our proper thinking about the meaning and personal implications of this subject is the needed follow-through of the theological sentence we are to write (following the ground-rules of the grammar of grace). The central word is "theology," *theo* (God) and *logos* (words about God's revelation to and for us). There is no real mystery here. We are trying to talk about God and do it carefully in light of God having first talked to us perfectly in Jesus Christ. There again is the Christian gospel in a nutshell.

So, that's essentially what's involved in doing theology. It is the task of carefully crafting a biblically-informed and Jesus-based sentence that clarifies our faith and focuses our mission. It has a *subject*—God gracefully for us in

Jesus—and an action *verb*—the Spirit of Jesus teaching, guiding, empowering, and sending us. And, best of all, it has a grateful *object*—you and me! And there is still more. There are other sentences to follow. The action Verb enables our own responding verbs, our acts of obedience as the Spirit's instruments of grace. The objects—the receivers of the Spirit's grace-full actions through us—will be the lost and hurting of our world.

So let's get to writing! Check to see how many chapters comprise the Book of Acts in the New Testament. To those twenty-eight, in a very important sense, are to come more, many more. They will be the ongoing acts of God through his newly grace-literate and Spirit-empowered writers—you and me, the church, Christ's family on mission. To be "theologians" is to be truly grace-literate believers actively seeking to understand and express to others the meanings and implications of God's grace for our truly knowing the redeeming acts of God and then truly living redemptively in this world.

Why does doing Christian theology have to get complicated? Well, we're trying to understand God, the One who is well beyond our understanding. We are trying at least to apprehend (if not comprehend) the nature, will, and ways of the incomprehensible One now shining before us in Jesus Christ. We are sitting on our little seashore of Earth and trying to count the number of drops in the watery expanse spread out before us. But that's not all. We are also trying to put what we have been given by divine revelation into language that makes sense to those who will hear us witness to it. And language keeps changing, as do whole cultures that need to be addressed. We have a huge subject and the demands of clear communication as we face our mission assignment of taking the good news to the whole world. That's Christian theology. It will never be fully or finally done, nor is it ever optional.

At least this much can be said, and it does help. How good it is that Jesus came! Without him we would be left to do so much unguided guessing. But we do have the Christ-Word to guide our words. And we do have the Spirit-breath to fill our lungs. We can be made alive by God's grace—which gives us a structure and dynamic for our thinking and living. It's God's grace grammar, and it's our writing assignment.

The Gospel of John tells the story of Jesus. This Gospel has been said to be so simple that anyone can get it right off. It also, even with its simplicity, is so profound that the greatest genius among us has barely scratched its surface. So it is with Jesus himself. How good it is that, when he went away, his Spirit came to be our ongoing teacher and guide. The Spirit is our reading and writing instructor, God remaining with us all the way.

So beware. We theologians, you and me, however bright and studious we are, will never become experts in our subject matter. We will merely touch the divine, and that only because the divine already has touched us. The touch is never everything there is, but it is enough for our knowing and writing and living needs. Do you know the extremely popular song by Bill Gaither titled "He Touched Me"? My now-deceased friend Doug Oldham moved crowds for many years by sharing vocally this song and amazing fact. Be a good theologian by first being touched and then by helping others to be touched by how carefully you explain your experience and their opportunity.

It is a known fact that children are hardly human in their development if not touched and cuddled by loving adults. All of us have been touched lovingly *by God*, our amazingly loving Parent. That touch has allowed us to be human in the fullest and most wonderful sense if we will receive the touch gratefully and faithfully. Here's the Gaither chorus:

> He touched me, O He touched me,
> And O the joy that floods my soul;
> Something happened, and now I know,
> He touched me and made me whole.

The new-life sentences we are enabled to construct and live because of God's touch (grace) are to be written according to God's special grammar, God's distinctive ways of communicating with our troubled world. They will never be complete sentences, at least not in this life, but they can be timely and good ones.

We who are touched by God—and thereby changed—begin through the Spirit to touch others with grace-full thinking and living. This grammar of grace follows the unusual rules of believing and living set up by God who was with us in Jesus, is still with us in the Spirit of Jesus, and will be with us always, even to the end of the age (Matt. 28:20). Write on!

Basic Assumptions

The grace-grammar of God features two central aspects to its revelation and redemption sentence, and to our responding "life sentences"—sounds like a long time in prison when it's actually a glorious forever in the lap of pure love. These aspects are the more stable fixedness of enduring truth, grace *nouns,* and the more motion-oriented and current mission elements of that truth, grace *verbs.* Both are very important in Christian theology. We are dealing with the God (*the* Noun) who has acted to redeem (past nouns) and the God who is a living Actor still generating current verbs. The Spirit of God blows where it chooses, convicting, renewing, teaching, and healing—all wonderful and very present grace verbs.

The unchanging realities (nouns) are critical, but are fewer in number than many believers have thought and insisted on. God is, Christ came, the Spirit remains—these are fundamental nouns on which all else is built. Particular church structures and practices and belief statements are time-bound, important but shifting as culture, language, and people move on. Walking with these theological nouns and verbs is a delicate and special work of art. Knowing what is a stable theological noun and what is a fluid theological verb is very important. Chapter ten is all about "which is which."

Here's a key point I hope you get for sure. The on-journey nature of verbs ought to be more typical than the many things we wrongly classify among the faith's fixed nouns. Admittedly, something not tied down causes an uncomfortable tension that tempts the believer to make a noun out of a verb (idolatry). We must keep the flexible from becoming rigid, an aliveness made into a set orthodoxy. We must not close prematurely what should be an "open" theology. To do so yields to our anxiety and need for security—and perverts truth in the process. There is a particular grammar to the revealing and working of the grace of God, and to the growing life of believers. We must be faithful to it and not short-circuit it.

A reporter once argued that Dwight D. Eisenhower was a greater president of the United States than Franklin D. Roosevelt. "Ike" supposedly could have gotten us out of the Great Depression more quickly than FDR, and without the need for the economic boost of a world war. Maybe, maybe not. Such speculation is pointless. Wondering if George Washington would have ended World War II without dropping the atomic bombs that Harry Truman did, or whether John F. Kennedy would have ended slavery more quickly that did Abraham Lincoln is a waste of good time.

Here's the simple fact. Each of us enters the ongoing history of this world at a specific point. We must "go with the flow" even while we seek to alter the course of things in a better direction. Some things are fixed (nouns) and some are not (verbs). Some things are eternal and some passing. Knowing the difference is of critical importance. It is a working skill of the mature theologian. We each bring our gifts to the times that swirl around us, times always in motion. We make decisions and exercise faith in a given context. We gather convictions while hoping to avoid idolatries. We act in faith and must not suppose that our words and actions are exactly those of God.

One important and constant question posed by a life of faith is this. What is there, if anything, that is *eternally stable* and *always true for everyone*? One might say that "theology" is asking this question seriously and learning how to adjust properly to whatever answer is found. It is much like composing a sentence. We must identify the actor, the action, and what best describes and qualifies the actor and the action. These components of the sentence interact to present a whole thought, a full picture of a reality first perceived in light of divine revelation and then proclaimed by us in the best ways we can. We receive faith's substance in one form (a given culture, language, set of institutions) and then we enter into a process of careful revision of its expressions and applications for a new place and time.

There is no good option—sorry. We must learn to be appropriate to our time and place, being simultaneously faithful to the fixed nouns and the flowing and ever-alive and flexible verbs of the faith and of our times. Such learning, and knowing which is which, is a big part of the business of Christian theology. The next chapter focuses on sorting out which is which. We must stay with the basics once we know what they are—and avoid an improper adding to the list because of our own anxiety and arrogance.

Would you prefer that theology take a simpler way, a way far more fixed than fluid, a way you don't have to work at, just memorize and recite? I know your likely answer, and I also would prefer the easier way. If all truth could be collected in a religious dictionary and looked up as needed, it would be a relief—and a mistake. To tie down an animal that should be allowed to move freely (like a dog tightly chained to a tree) is abuse. It also is bad theological business to close the door to further thought and freshly relevant ways to express old truths. It's arrogance, idolatry, and selfish security. It's done all the time by good people who really love Jesus but don't want to deal with questions and doubts.

Christian theology is a biblically-informed and God-based collection of sentences with a few fixed nouns and numerous fluid verbs. It is *theo—logos*, carefully chosen words about this ultimate One (*theo*) and Spirit-led reflection on the resulting meanings of these words for our ever-changing lives and times and truth understandings (*logos*). The words must be ordered in a way appropriate to the beginning assumption of God now come in Jesus Christ. And they must be enlivened by the ongoing and ever present work of Christ's Spirit.

In these pages there is a fundamental assumption being made. God as biblically presented is loving, relational, reaching, and redeeming; therefore, there is a special *grammar of grace* that must guide the writing of our faith and the living of our faith lives. It necessarily follows the rules set down by our grace-enabled understanding of the God who is, who has, and who continues to be the God of loving grace.

Theologically speaking, the current times in the Christian world are marked by a clash of "grammar" preferences. Too much emphasis is being placed on claimed nouns when that emphasis really should be on vital verbs. My recommended theological style will be a more verb-oriented approach to the faith. It is a "process" preference.[27] Key nouns are always assumed, but they are not many. The point of faith is to stand on these and come alive in the verb world—receiving, being changed, writing new Spirit sentences, and activating the Spirit's mission.

Kid Talk, God Talk

A provocative book titled *Vernacular Eloquence* argues that every speaker of a language has in his or her head a set of rules for using that language.[28] Initially, this "grammar" is acquired by hearing and observing other speakers. Much of this language work is done in the earliest years of life. Language learning later in life comes to involve a greater degree of explicit instruction in the "proper" (socially accepted) manner of speaking and writing of the language. Often this proper way is in some conflict with what has been known and used since childhood--to the consternation of language teachers and students alike. "Street" language and book language can present some crude contrasts.

The situation is similar when it comes to learning the grammar of Christian theology. We do some of it when barely out of our cribs. We hear parents and pastors "doing" theology with comments, body language, and attitudes. We learn what apparently is right, acceptable, and workable before we do much thinking for ourselves. It happens in our homes and churches, and even on the streets and playgrounds. Some of us then go to a Bible college or Christian university or seminary and encounter more formal standards, rules, and traditions of theological construction. Yes, we learn about multiple traditions inside Christianity, sometimes competing grammars even within the one faith. Some of them are quite rigid and unfortunately have a high degree of assurance about the fixedness and final correctness of many things. Some are much more flexible.

So the obvious question arises. When faced with formalized instruction of the faith's *proper* grammar, proper by someone's judgment, what do we do? Do we abandon the "natural," what has been homebound, instinctual, and experiential, for the more formal, critical, and highly ordered approach to our theological grammar? Are the two inherent enemies, the language we bring from our homes and in our hearts and the one found in the textbooks with carefully developed rules, footnotes, bibliographies, and required outcomes? Does one or the other have to go? Can—should—they be mixed? If so, how? Now you begin to see why theology can get complicated and confusing.

There certainly is a wide range of speaking/writing styles today. Rappers create as they go while doctoral candidates become slaves to highly structured writing styles. Text messages and tweets use an array of abbreviations for about everything. So much of it is speaking to a screen rather than to each other directly. The New Testament struggles with this very thing—how to relate the rather fixed "Law" known to the Jews to the more spontaneous and person-oriented law of love emphasized by Jesus. Love is said to fulfill law, sometimes without following strictly the Law's set traditions (sabbath breaking, etc.) This got Jesus and Paul into plenty of trouble. Religious establishments prefer a high level of fixedness.

"Correct" writing is rarely our mother tongue. Highly reasoned theology textbooks are hardly where most believers begin their spiritual journeys. So, is the formalized and carefully controlled kind of language (theology) the best? Yes, but not exclusively. Kid-talk has a wisdom of its own. Out of the mouths of babes.... Our out-of-classroom language carries a richness of feeling and instinct that can enrich formal writing without destroying its correctness.

I once listened patiently to a revivalist preach from a particular biblical text. According to the rules of interpretation I learned in seminary, he was butchering badly what the text really said in its context. Even so, he had a heart of gold and was offering himself and his understanding to God's Spirit as an instrument of grace for needy people. His formal grammar was highly suspect, but his grace grammar was rich and fruitful. Many responded in life-changing ways to what he had to say—or apparently what God was saying through him despite himself. The lesson for me—and you? While we gather our academic credentials, and this is good, we had better keep our humility in tact. The Spirit blows where it will!

Careful writing, Bible reading, and preaching (paradoxically) can be improved with the calculated addition of "careless" speech--with both benefitting in the process. The dynamic of God's Spirit is essential to a fully adequate God language. There are essential nouns, but they come alive with real meaning and are truly themselves to us only in the presence of Spirit-pulsing verbs of being and loving. That's what Jesus kept trying to say about the Jewish Law. His words fell on many deaf ears. I hope that yours are open.

Even so, with the Spirit pulsing in our thoughts and beliefs, not just anything goes. There are a few sure words on which all else must hang. We now turn to what they are and quickly learn that even the most stable and fixed of truths in the Christian faith sometimes come in paradoxical form.

9

FIXED AND FLUID

*Question: Is theology definite or not, changing or unchanging?
Yes!*

Please, not paradoxes! They're confusing, messy, surely running from the simple, plain truth. Many conservative critics of formalized theologies make this accusation. They are wrong. Paradoxes are everywhere—and at points very important to mature Christian theology. The fact is that "Christianity pivots on paradox.... There are two sides to every story.... It is time to land with both feet on the ground, with both sides of the paradox carrying equal weight."[29]

Paradox Alert!

A 2013 issue of the *Christian Science Monitor* news magazine featured the theme of high-tech spying among today's nations. It was prompted by a recent revelation that the United States was spying even on its European allies—creating some awkward international feelings. The story was begun with "Paradox Alert." The situation was similar to so much in the world of Christian theology.

Half of the world was outraged by governments conducting massive eavesdropping on hundreds of millions of people without their knowledge—a terrible intrusion on privacy. The other half of the world, meanwhile, "was blithely posting intimate details of their private lives on Facebook, Twitter, and other social media." Half prized privacy as a sacred right; the other half recklessly broadcast everything, no matter how intimate or inane as though privacy was a meaningless abstraction.

What's the paradox here? To know the real world requires realizing the presence of both halves that make up this crazy place in all its complexity. Big truths usually have many parts, interlocking to form one whole. If a coin has two sides and still is just one coin, why can't theology be paradoxical? Keep in mind that half of the truth can be worse than no truth at all. To avoid all of the truth is to lie with part of the truth. "Heresy" (a bad deviation from the truth) often is no more than grasping part of a truth and parading it as the whole thing. Kids do this all the time.

"Did you finally clean up your room, Sarah?"

"Yes, Mom, I sure did!" And she had, but by pushing everything under the bed and randomly tossing out of sight in the closet what wouldn't fit under the bed. The room now looked great at a glance, but it wasn't, not really. The whole truth was that there now were clean floors—clean because the junk had been hastily moved under the bed and into the closet. Sarah was right—and wrong. The room was now clean—and still dirty. How like us paradoxical humans!

There are several paradoxes in the world of Christian theology, some quite uncomfortable. Here's one. We theological hopefuls must be careful about putting exclamation points after our theological convictions. Many of them don't deserve that much emphasis. On the other hand, to believe only a little and not ever be ready to bet your life on anything, to put an exclamation point nowhere, isn't good either. The divine announcement to the church in Laodicea was: "I know your works; you are neither cold nor hot.... So I am about to spit you out of my mouth" (Rev. 3:15-16). Not good! We must be cautious in our believing, and yet really believe something—hopefully the right something, and in its wholeness and with deep conviction.

Here's a simple fact. There is a wide range of belief among Christians of differing cultures, centuries, and denominations. Is diversity of belief a disaster or an enrichment? Could contrasting beliefs be worthy parts of one whole? Are some beliefs optional and others mandatory in order to be a real Christian? If there are two categories of belief, optional and not optional, what beliefs fit into which category?

In fact, likely there are really three categories facing Christian theologians. The pressing question is how we can sort out (1) what is absolutely essential, (2) what is important but not essential, and (3) what can be left in the "who cares" category of allowable personal opinion (these three categories will be defined more carefully in the next chapter). How can we be sure that letting something go may be losing a piece of something that is really important? How can we avoid making idols out of unworthy things? How can we avoid breaking a sacred paradox by denying something essential and thus wandering into the jungle of heresy?

<u>Levels of Doctrinal Importance</u>

A	B	C
Absolutely Essential	Important but Not Essential	Open to Our Personal Choices

Let's highlight this problem with an instance where the appropriate category was rather clear. A seminary student who later turned into a famous Christian theologian was struggling with a writing assignment on the doctrine of the Trinity (the three-ness of the one God—got that big paradox?). The doorbell rang. It was a Jehovah's Witness missionary making his rounds in the neighborhood. The student invited him in and they talked for over two hours about matters of the deity of Christ, salvation by grace through faith, and God's *tri-unity*. The conversation came to a sudden end when the seminarian suggested that they pray together. The visitor got up and left quickly, announcing with some drama that prayer wasn't acceptable because they wouldn't be addressing the same God![30]

I suggest at a minimum that it is essential to have the same God in view when we approach prayer or theology—and the Christian understanding of God does involve a tri-unity (I will help you with this later). Having said that, we also can say that much beyond the existence and essential nature of God will have to be sorted out and categorized very carefully. Here is an example of the problem.

I have been in discussions among Christians where the "eschatological" (end-time) schemes of pre-millenialism, post-millenialism, and a-millenialism were heatedly at issue. Some were committed strongly to one or another of these views of interpreting the Book of Revelation—all claiming to be fully biblical. Some weren't sure what these words even meant and wondered if it made any difference which was right—if any.

Should Christians baptize by sprinkling, pouring, or immersing? Adults only or babies? Are the answers important? Many Christians are very concerned that the Bible can be read so differently by sincere believers. We have such a tendency to read *into* the biblical text rather than *out of* it. In light of many such things that sometimes perplex and divide Christians, and remembering that there are three available categories for doctrinal subjects, let's learn a lesson from the heavens above—putting a little astronomy into our theology.

The Sun and the Planets

It couldn't have been missed even if only a coincidence. My wife and I were vacationing in one of the beauty spots of the world, the little town of Geiranger that sits snuggled at the end of a picturesque Norwegian fjord. We spent the afternoon in our stateroom on a large cruise ship anchored in the harbor watching the tenders come and go to shore, transporting many of our cruising crowd to the waiting shops and tour buses. That's when the coincidence happened. The relentless transporting of curious people was the expected agenda of this day. What suddenly caught our attention, however, were the rock walls that towered around us.

The surrounding walls were huge, stable, motionless, the fixed setting in which we fragile and temporary humans flitted to and fro. Then the television in our stateroom began airing a documentary on Galileo, that seventeenth-century Italian who decided that the church was wrong in its teaching of the earth's absolute fixedness in the universe. His experiments had told him that, quite surprisingly, the earth is actually in constant motion. It is the sun that is the center of our universe, with the planets the wandering tourists circling about its central stability. This dramatic conclusion created an unpleasant clash of tradition and novelty, of faith and reason, of church interpretation and contrary conclusions of science. Galileo paid the price of being ahead of his time.

There lies an enduring issue in Christian theology. What is the noun and what is the verb. What holds still and what moves? What acts and what is acted upon? What is the fixed and unmovable center, and what is in motion about it? Our human senses cannot always be trusted to answer properly. Established beliefs can be as wrong as they are old. Our reasoning is crucial, but hardly definitive because it must work from assumptions based on what information we happen to have. There may be more to life and Christian belief than logic can predict or contain or properly identify.

There are shifting contexts in which Christian believers seek to understand and express their faith. There are words with various meanings and differing traditions of Christian understanding. Even so, movement on multiple fronts does not mean—I hope--that all belief is contextual, shifting, merely personal preference or the product of time and place. Much of the thought now in vogue highlights the immediate and contextual. This is important, and yet it does not eliminate the enduring grounding in which "orthodox" belief is to be rooted. We will look at this as the relationship between *fixed* nouns and *fluid verbs*—and do it with an eye to not cursing.

When it comes to Christians and theology, a considerable amount of "cursing" goes on. I don't mean a mere flow of vulgar words, but the void of *just not caring*. The Hebrew word is *qalal*. It means to make light, judge something to have little weight, to be of marginal importance. Exercised harshly, it can mean to "curse." Done more gently, but just as devastatingly, it can mean to ignore, to dishonor by giving something or someone the status of being next to nothing. To make trivial may be the worst form of cursing. Many Christians are uninformed and even hostile toward the very subject of theology. I find this situation appalling, truly dangerous to the future of the church. I join honored colleagues Stanley J. Grenz and Roger E. Olson in fearing that Christianity may be in danger of becoming a mere "folk religion," relegated to the "realms of sheer subjectivity and emptied of public credibility." The result will be a body of Christians who "lack theological literacy and acumen" and thus in their self-chosen ignorance are "tossed about by every wind of doctrine that comes sweeping through our media-dominated culture."[31] Is that you?

To choose the rudeness and shallowness of *qalal* is to risk emptying oneself. A dishonoring attitude toward theology soon turns to a painful dishonoring of the integrity of one's own belief claims and life practices. It is to insist that the language of the Christian faith has no necessary "grammar," structural integrity, rules that govern what is proper and what is not, what is true and what is not. It's all a personal matter to be structured as we choose, or to leave unstructured altogether.

Here's how it really is. Christian belief and life are comprised of a combination of factors. Achieving the best balance among them is a significant goal of the work of Christian theology. First, Christianity is rooted in a given history, that of Israel, Jesus, and the early church. No other history is of equal importance in truly understanding the faith. Second, Christian belief always is in the process of moving in the midst of particular times. It necessarily adapts as it goes, but it should not adapt to the degree of uprooting its historic foundations. This is a delicate balance that always lies at the heart of theological work. Be rooted, and be relevant; honor yesterday, but live in today.

Two skilled Christian scholars have traced the centuries between the time of Jesus and today and noticed a recurring pendulum effect in prevailing Christian thought.[32] Patterns of belief have swung one way and then another. There always is the motion of this swinging, and there also persists a drawing back to the more stable center. The driving force often has been an attempted correction, one group seeing the weakness of the recent past and choosing to head the other way to make things right again—only to go too far and set the stage for a later group wanting to correct them with a new reversing of course. The challenges before would-be reformers often are real, significant, and timely. These challenges tend to be tackled vigorously, with the alternative stated, likely overstated, bringing change, and eventually becoming the subject of more change. On and on the swinging goes. On and on the center seeks to hold.

One key characteristic of the constant change has involved a move from a focus on the relatively *fixed* to the more *fluid*, and then back again. Creeds, denominations, and traditions become standard, routine, rationalized, institutionalized, taken for granted, expected of all. I'm thinking of the fixed as nouns. Faith's nouns sometimes grow very large while the more flexible verbs shrink into a passive mode, jumbling the church's sentences. Dissatisfied believers eventually start reaching for the more personal, dynamic, fresh, fluid. They call for the freedom of the Spirit of God. The pendulum swings, helpfully but maybe too far. An ice-age of the excessively fixed is allowed to melt in the Spirit's heat. The lava flows bright red again, but even it soon cools and hardens.

Corrective reform movements that have leaned to the side of fresh fluidity in Christian belief have carried many names over the centuries. Included most recently are Pietism, Pentecostalism, Process philosophy/theology, and Post-modernism. Each, in different times and settings and with somewhat differing emphases, has reached for a dynamic newness, a more personal, relational, sometimes individualistic and even a mystical way of conceiving and appropriating the faith. They have brought new life and vigor and sense of relevance into the Christian community. They also have brought their distinctive vulnerabilities.

Clearly, there has been an ongoing process of reformers seeking change and then those who want to reform the reformers. Theology needs mediators who are sensitive about the need for balance and the role of paradox in believing.[33] Must we always be in danger of one extreme or the other? Are you open to seeking balance, wholeness, freshness without the need to eliminate the good of yesterday?

Good theology is a delicate balancing act. There is believing and doubting, being sure and yet staying open to new or corrected truth perceptions. After all, our belief is always based on our faith in the best information we have. It is important to resist the all-yes/all-no, either/or mindset. Our theological eyes must remain open wide enough to see the importance of both the *fixed* and the *fluid*. We must be careful grammarians who insist on *complete* theological sentences, with all parts of speech present and playing their proper roles.

It has been argued that Christian theology, at least in intellectual circles, is viewed as being one of two general types. One is "conservative" and the other "liberal." The first appeals to supernatural revelation that is fixed and stands beyond the scrutiny of human intellectual disciplines. The second is much more fluid and "avoids contradicting modern historical and scientific knowledge by not asserting anything significant."[34] It tends to put a religious gloss over secularism's God-denying view of reality. Good theology can't be allowed to strangle in the mire of either of these extreme options.

Where Am "I"?

If only the two categories existed (conservative or liberal as defined above), I probably would lean toward the conservative. Since things aren't quite that restrictive, however, I intend to lie somewhere to the *progressive side of the middle*. I join a line of reformers who have tried to champion the more *fluid* over the excessively *fixed* in Christian believing—but without denying that some fixedness is essential for the integrity of the faith.

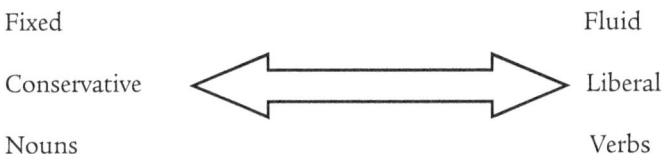

Such a reform effort appears timely again as rigid fundamentalisms (the highly fixed people) grip religious communities worldwide. However, you and I must be careful about our own excess, knowing that our critics already are waiting in the wings should we go too far. Such is the way of things in the fluctuating grammar of Christian theology.

There is another key choice to make beyond the fixed-fluid or conservative-liberal continuum. It is the delicate but critical choice between a focus on either "I" or "It." Be sure of this. We are not playing a silly game of--Do I want a "t" after my "I" or not? If on the first set of choices I stand on the progressive side of the middle, on this one I am all the way to the left. I am a theological "I" person and hope you will be too. Let me explain.

Martin Buber (d.1965) was a Jewish philosopher known for his distinction between *I–Thou* and *I–It* relationships, viewing all other persons either as genuine persons to value (Thou) or as things to use (It). All real living is "meeting," he insisted. To view another person as a thing makes true meetings impossible. Our human prejudices, racisms, nationalisms, and even formalized religions too often encourage us to make "things" of people, especially the one who are unlike us.

Attitudes of condescension reduce the "unfit" (the "heretics") to a status below ourselves, destroying dialogue, true meeting, real conversation. We then talk *at* and not *with* others. So, who are the holy people a viewed by the Christian theological tradition? They are the ones who are separated from the crowd by God and empowered by the Spirit to imitate Jesus by initiating true and loving conversations. Being like Jesus transforms hostility into peace by true self-giving love expressed in vulnerable and redemptive exchanges with others. The holy ones are not the perfect performers who have the whole truth on their side. They are the loving and redeeming and relating ones.

Some Christian evangelists have been guilty of severe condescension, speaking sharply at "sinners," even ones they do not know personally, and demanding that they repent or else! There is no meeting, no person-to-person contact, no I-Thou conversation in such speaking. There is mostly the threat of hell if there is no agreement and repentance. By contrast, Jesus gave himself to a ministry of dialogue, treating even his opponents as persons of worth in God's eyes. They were worthy of his personal time and the risking of his own life for the sake of theirs.

Jesus took risks to be with people in serious conservation--tax collectors, prostitutes, fishermen, Samaritans, people quite unlike himself. To him, they were "I" people, not "Its" (things to be avoided, even used). The Jews of his day often avoided such people as unworthy. But Jesus connected and spoke truth in love, always having proper regard for the person to whom he was speaking—and, of course, in time he was made to pay the ultimate price by the offended, the fixed and intolerant religious "establishment" and occupying power (Rome).

The coming of Jesus has highlighted this *I-Thou* insight as central to who God is and how God chooses to relate to us humans, now a spoiled creation. The cross of Jesus is a dramatic symbol of God's Self-revelation. God did not throw us terrible sinners to our knees with a display of judgmental power. Rather, he opened to us his bleeding heart while we were yet sinners (Rom. 5:8). He lovingly invited us to listen, respond, and choose freely to turn from our sin and be made wonderfully new. Rather than the threat of hell hurled at us came a gentle invitation to new creation and holiness. Our freedom to choose was not violated, our dignity as persons not overrun. For the sake of our salvation, love took the costly risk of being rejected. The relational God created us in love and continues to relate to us lovingly.

East or West?

In a theological sense, the Christian world has been divided for centuries. Which is right, Roman Catholic or Protestant, East or West? The answer is-- Yes (a paradox). Sorry.

The directional East-West divide has split the Christian world since 1054. It is the divide associated with Constantinople (the "orthodox" churches of the East) and Rome (the Roman Catholic and Protestant churches of the West). The split is less a geographic phenomenon and more a divergence in styles of conceiving select perceptions, doctrines, and practices of Christian faith. The rupture is sometimes considered in the East as a basic tragedy in Christian church history through which the West has lost its theological and spiritual balance.[35] The West, of course, sees it otherwise. They are both wrong—and, of course, they are both partly right.

This serious divide can be characterized in various ways. One is the "therapy" or healing way that the East tends to understand human salvation, in contrast to the West's tendency to employ more "legalistic" categories, a reflection of ancient Roman "law" dominant for so long. The Western way has been heightened by the emphasis of the modern world on the power of human reason and the scientific approach to gathering "facts" to support the best theories currently available. But the way of the East persists in its focusing somewhat differently.

The Eastern way of Christianity is a corrective to the West in ways reflective of what this book now is attempting in relation to much of contemporary "evangelical" Christianity in the West. Christianity will not be understood here as having the task or ability to bring clear and rationalized answers to many of the questions that believers and the "world" routinely pose. By contrast, the faith will be understood as making believers progressively aware of a mystery. God "is not so much the object of our knowledge as the cause of our wonder.... [Our faith] helps us to reach out beyond all statements positive or negative, beyond all language and all thought, towards an immediate experience of the living God.... It is to know God not as a theory or an abstract principle, but as a person.... Our [Eastern Orthodox] way of entry into the mystery of God is through personal love."[36]

One theologian of the West, John Wesley, shows considerable affinity with the Eastern faith perception.[37] As a "practical" theologian, he emphasized "perfect love" as the ideal of "sanctified" Christian believers. He insisted that, in addition to a fixed "orthodoxy," there must be an experiential dimension to true religion. It dare not be rigidly scholastic or institutional, not a noun dominance, but a greater transforming potential found in the living, more verb-like *I-Thou*.[38]

Thinking in grammatical terms, Wesley and the East in general do not entirely eliminate the structures and rules of ordered faith or the meaningfulness of established language like church creeds. They do not leap into the irrational, but exhibit clear recognition of the radical limitations of human reason and conceptual language. They point us to "a way beyond the arid rationalism that threatens much of our Western secular culture and even some of our theologies.... The great mysteries of the faith are for the East matters of *adoration* rather than *analysis*. The creeds *describe* rather than *dissect* the great truths of Christianity...."[39] The truth is that we need some of both. Even so, as I lean to the progressive side of the conservative-liberal paradox, I also lean a little eastward.

10

WHICH IS WHICH?

Question: Two or four? Is theology some kind of math game? And what about tradition, reason and/or spiritual experience? Must we choose?

I'm sorry to bring this up, but I must. If nouns represent the stable side of theological things, you should be aware that some nouns are less stable than others. A big theological task is deciding which are the enduring truth nouns, the basic, stable, and essential ones, and which are less so. And beyond the two styles of nouns, there also are the verbs. They are the more dynamic and fluid realities of being and action. But which are which? Which are nouns and which verbs? And which nouns are essential and which are not? Critical mistakes in identification are made all the time and can have serious consequences for believers, their churches, and the mission of Christ in the world.

Only Two Things to Do

One essential and very stable faith noun for Christians is belief in the final rightness of clear biblical teaching. Christians should affirm the Bible as the treasured deposit of God's revelation to us, the most dependable place where God speaks and we should listen. But even here we face the dilemma of competing interpretations of the meaning of the sacred text. Unfortunately, a little of the fluid emerges right in the middle of the most fixed. Even so, the biblical base is always our return point and it is much more stable than fluid.

Once having accepted the Bible-base assumption, choosing to be informed and "inspired" (God-breathed revelation) from above, we move on into the big world of the church's thinking over the centuries about what the Bible teaches and what to do with its teachings once identified. Here we find two relatively consistent theological tasks. Each has at least one fundamental challenge. These tasks and challenges make up the heart of what it means to do theology and do it well. I would like to cover all this ground with you more simply, but that would be simplistic—and that is unacceptable.

Here is the overall picture as plainly as I can put it. Good theology must always be doing two things—with one of them having three parts.

- **Task A** is in the *noun* world. It is rediscovering and reaffirming the basic foundations (nouns) of the faith. What are the historic roots and enduring substance of the Christian faith? The believer must come to know the heart of the faith.

- **Task B** is in the *verb* world. It is re-conceiving, re-wording, and re-living (three great verbs) the faith's foundations in currently understandable and relevant ways. The concern is for communication and witness. Our world needs to hear, see, and understand this faith.

There is the two-part theological roadmap, the historic noun world and the contemporary verb world, what the faith is and what we should become and do with it. I know that it's easier to say than to do, but the theological roadmap does have only two parts, each with its big challenge.

The two basic parts of doing Christian theology might be put this way: "Theology moves back and forth between two poles, the eternal truth of its foundation and the temporal situation in which the eternal truth must be received [and conveyed]."[40] What is the truth and what must I do with it? What is the good news and how do I absorb it into my life and put it in fresh language that really communicates today? What is *truly Christian* and how can I word and live the truth so that it is *truly relevant* for me and others? Clear enough?

If clear, then I need to make it just a little more complex—sorry. Identifying the whats and hows is where things get sticky, where the debates and divisions come in. I will guide you into and through this quagmire the best I can. To begin, we obviously need some immediate clarity on the three aspects of the first big task. Remember that I said **Task A** has three sub-parts.

The fact is that some beliefs are more important—more fixed, stable, enduring—than others. Theological nouns tend to be very significant to us, but they should be more or less so depending on what they are. They come in three categories.

- a. **Essential to the gospel of Christ**. Some theological nouns should come in all capital letters. They are that important, that basic. Without them the theological sentence we attempt to write will not be true Christianity. Failing to affirm these truth nouns is to fall off the theological wagon and reject the faith itself. Nouns of this kind are relatively few, but exceedingly important.

    There are a few beliefs—very few--that all Christians must hold if they are to be Christians at all. I will not elaborate here since that is what chapter eleven is about. I will say only this for now. Accepting the full lordship of Jesus Christ as explained biblically is the lead noun, the essential of essentials. Take this away from the "good news" and there is no good news that can be called "Christian."

- b. **Important but not essential for every believer**. Most Christian traditions (denominations) champion one or more teachings that they judge really important and not held adequately by other believers. While they usually do not go so far as to say that failure to hold such teachings ruins the faith for the others, they do not hesitate to make them litmus tests for membership in their particular bodies of believers. To be "one of us," you must be baptized a certain way (sprinkled, poured, immersed, as a baby or an adult) or believe that serving the Lord's Supper is basic to any and every Christian worship service or subscribe to a dispensational view of church history and final things, or...or....

    By the way, if you haven't the slightest idea what the dispensational view is, you're probably in a Christian group that doesn't consider it particularly important or even thinks it wrong. Denominations usually take the approach that matters important to their particular understanding of the faith, but not absolutely essential for all Christians to hold, will not send anyone to hell if not believed.

c. Interesting and helpful, but maybe only to you and only for now. We all have opinions and passing perspectives on many matters. When we are at this relatively unimportant level, we must be careful not to push on others our private perspectives. They are of no more value that the information on which they are based and on whether or not they ring true in light of biblical revelation.

OK, so there are only two basic things to do in the theological enterprise and, unfortunately, the first of them has three parts. A big task, then, is figuring out which of the three we are dealing with when a particular subject presents itself. To sort out the three, we need a four-part strategy—theology is a little like a math problem. If grammar didn't get you, maybe this math will. You must take the risk. Things are as they are.

A Quadrilateral (what's that?)

Here's an irony. We want theology to be in plain language and now I bring up a word with thirteen letters (quadrilateral). Well, it's because this word is critical when it comes to our reading and understanding the Bible. I want for us what John Wesley wanted for his early followers in England back in the 1700s. First, there should be high confidence in the authority of this book for Christian believers. The Bible comes to us through human hands, of course, but also with the inspiration of God's Spirit—people wrote while God was breathing on their writing so that somehow the result became more than just their faulty thoughts and stammering words. Amazing! Believing this is essential to Christianity.

What comes second after treasuring the dependable wisdom of the Bible? With the in-breathed writing must come our wise reading. We also must be in-breathed by the same Spirit so that the One who inspired these many biblical lines now inspires us to read so that we get the originally intended understanding in our own terms and for our own times.

How can we read properly this large and sometimes strange library of little books that have combined into one Bible? I want for us the same bottom line that John Wesley wanted long ago—"plain truth for plain people." Here's the irony we wish weren't the case. Being plain is plainly not easy. We come to our reading of God's Word with our own perspectives, biases, and agendas, and with our limited knowledge of the ancient languages and cultures that are so basic to the Bible's origin and nature—a tough beginning.

Can you define for me the distinctive nature of "apocalyptic" literature (be very careful when trying to interpret the book of Revelation if you can't). Can you tell for sure whether or not the "majestic plural" in ancient Hebrew implies the Trinity of God's eternal nature? You're somebody special if you can. Are you up to speed on the word "hermeneutics"? That's what we're talking about here, the "science" of biblical interpretation. The word is unimportant, but not what it involves.

The need for a "quadrilateral" in hermeneutics comes from a simple fact. We humans learn things in various ways and need checks and balances to be sure that what we think we know is not just coming from our own preference or ignorance. The quad is really a three-pronged approach to quality Bible reading and understanding. It is a system of checks and balances.

Let's be clear. A quadrilateral sounds like a four-sided something. However, this quad is not exactly four-sided—how confusing is that? The Bible is basic, unique as an authority source for Christians. But there are always three other things that belong on the reading table, each very important as an aid to reading the Bible well. Lacking good use of any one of the three can lead to serious error. So the quad is made up of the one (Bible), the written witness to divine revelation, plus the three that are interactive guides to reading the Bible well. These guides to understanding, these checks and balances against misunderstanding, are:

Tradition....a reading and remembering community (the church's legacy of interpretation— no need to always reinvent the wheel). There is a body of gathered wisdom waiting for you to draw upon.

Reason....testing for coherence of thought and its relatedness to all other wisdom known (don't park your brain at the door, and know that God's wisdom relates naturally to all other wisdom).

Experience....experiencing personally the impact of the revelation (some things are only known well from the inside).

What have other believers thought? What makes sense in light of my best thinking? What is self-authenticating in my own life as a believing reader? We must not read the sacred text disinterestedly, in isolation from our brothers and sisters, or with our brains unplugged.

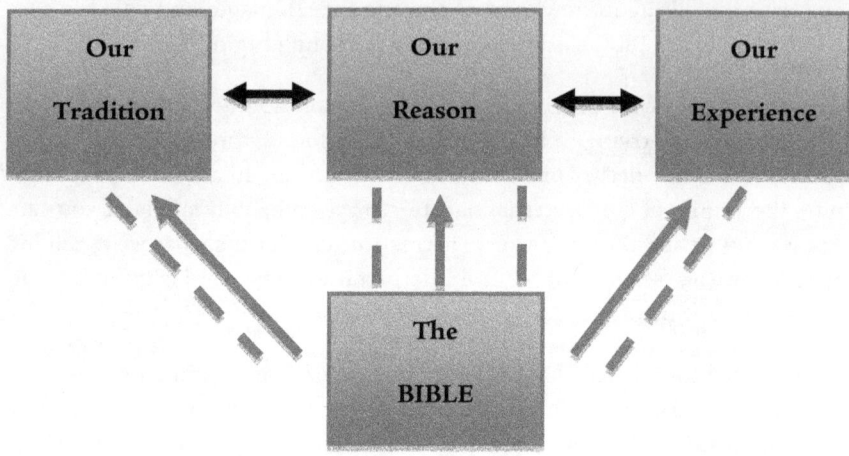

So, we get the quad idea by taking these three and adding the Bible—or better, taking the Bible and bringing these three to bear as tools of adequate understanding of the biblical text. Note that the Bible should send revealed wisdom to our mixed traditions, fallen reason, and sometimes undependable experiences (the strong arrows of authority in the graphic). But wisdom goes the other way too (the dashed lines). We necessarily read and interpret the Bible in a given setting (our tradition), with our available information and best logic (reason), and in light of our own life events, spiritual and otherwise (experience).

And don't forget something else that is very important. God's Spirit is always present and prepared to work through all of these quad parts. The Spirit inspired (breathed wisdom) into the original biblical text and now wants to illuminate (shower light) on our present path as we seek, in light of tradition, reason, and experience, to recover the original biblical wisdom in ways relevant to our own time and setting. The quad is a picture of the big theological task as these elements interact and seek fresh understanding of the voice of God now speaking.

Think of a baseball field (a sports quadrilateral). Everyone knows that to score a runner must safely touch all four bases, the last being home plate. In the Christian quest for understanding, home plate is the Bible, the ultimate authority, the place where real scoring happens, the best place to locate God's revealed wisdom. But to achieve adequate biblical understanding that is historically correct, currently relevant, and more from God than from us, one must touch three other bases on the way to understanding truth (scoring).

Relying mainly on any one of the quad parts in isolation from the others is a mistake—unfortunately, a very common one. To say (using experience mainly), "I feel that this is true because it warms me inside and gives me hope" is a wonderful thing to be able to say, but it easily could be all wrong. The fact is that, with my eyes closed, I can be comforted by feeling the strength of a smooth rope when, in fact, it is a poisonous snake. A wise man in Christian higher education—trying to convince a skeptical church of the importance of reason in the faith journey—once said this:

> Faith without reason is an ally of theological dogmatism and religious suerstition, bosom friends of error. But reason without faith is rationalism, which assumes that all reality must be verified, an assumption which is itself unreasonable. This universe is so vast and full of mystery that human reason alone is a puny instrument with which to relate ourselves to it. And the wider our scope of knowledge becomes the more the mystery deepens.[41]

Feel-good religion may be good in some ways—and wrong. Thoughtless religion may demand little of us—and be wrong. Wisdom lies in the discipline of wholeness. Read, remember, think, and be open to experiencing the quiet speaking of God's Spirit.

Toward Dynamic Verbs

I was crossing the Pacific Ocean when writing this chapter. We had people aboard the ship from some fifty nations, but we were one community eating, playing, and learning together. Clothes differed, languages differed, and faith convictions were various. But with all the diversity, we were spared the suicide bombers who make glaring statements of their faith and political convictions at the horrible expense of others. We encountered no aggressive "fundamentalists." Live and let live was the order of the day.

A fundamentalist removes the "fun" and "mental" from the faith, insisting on a pre-set compliance with the truth as they know it and not tolerating the independent thinker. Today's fundamentalists, whether Hindu, Islamic, Jewish, or Christian, are reacting in a protective way to the radical pluralism that marks our day. When common thought tolerates just about anything that wants to call itself truth, they are reacting with their own brands of "NO! Truth is truth, period!"

I understand this reaction, and I echo it to a point. More of me, however, wants to counter the extremes of the fundamentalists. In the name of defending the integrity of one's faith, we religious people easily overreact and compromise the faith's integrity by our own extremes. Our theological sentences get reduced to sharp expletives. Our grammar deteriorates into giant nouns of our own confessions and glaring adjectives demeaning the confessions of others. We forget that our faith is *by faith* and we know only *in part*.

The primary pioneer of my own Christian tradition cried out against "sectarianism," a divisive hardening of the church's arteries into fixed, arrogant, and competitive church groups. He insisted that the church is God's and we must be humble enough to allow the dynamic of the Spirit to rule. Since his time, the walls of denominationalism have lowered. Hardened creeds and arrogant denominations are now widely recognized to be destructive of Christian mission. Even so, new sectarianisms have arisen. This book is my anti-sectarian cry, hopefully not one louder than justified, but loud enough to be heard and, I hope, heeded.

My intended pendulum swing is in the direction of *dynamic verbs*. I am hoping you will avoid the downsides of inappropriately fossilized nouns of Christian believing and living. Rather than categorizing the theological options as left or right, liberal or conservative, fundamentalist or reformist, I choose the grammar option, the balanced interplay of verbs and nouns. Granted, verbs should never entirely *replace* nouns; however, verbs should keep faith's nouns appropriately flexible, humble, matters of faith, human things seeking to represent well the divine in our midst.

The medium of theological expression I am using here is grammar, the art of effective language construction and flow. There is a rhythm to effective language composition. Yes, there are rules. There also is an unwritten dynamic that engenders the richest meaning of the rules. The regulated construction of prose can yield to the less regulated beauty of poetry. Both have a place. The New Testament displays on nearly every page the efforts of Jesus, Paul, and others to permeate "law" with love.

The dynamic of compassion surrounds and tempers the strict and rigid faith nouns of the tradition that Jesus inherited. His intent was not to replace that tradition but to infuse it with the fresh life of God's original intention. Jesus was a verb man in a fixed world of sectarian nouns—and he is our theological mentor.

11

THE ESSENTIAL NOUNS

Question: Can you draw a theological map that has one fixed point from which four lines shoot out in fixed and yet changing ways? If you can, you can be a good theologian!

Fossilized theological nouns are a constant problem in church life. Even so, some nouns are not optional. They are fixed without being inappropriately fossilized. We must risk the fossilized in order to find the essential—and the last chapter provided guidelines on how to sort out which is which. I want to share with you the results of my sorting. Using the quadrilateral (see the previous chapter), my sorting has yielded what I consider the "orthodox" nouns, the few truths that the Christian tradition as a whole has always affirmed as truly biblical, reasonable, non-negotiable, and spiritually satisfying.

The Bottom Line

The bottom line, the enduring subjects of all truly Christian theological sentences, is distilled from what underlies the entire biblical text. Only a few core beliefs are basic and enduring from Genesis to Revelation, from the first to the twenty-first centuries. They should be the heart of Christian believing and teaching from the coming of the Spirit in the first century to the final coming of the Christ—whenever that will be.

The place to begin is the *subject* of every good and truly Christian theological sentence that we try to write—and construct. Who or what is acting on us and our world—in fact, who is the origin and destiny of all creation? We are used to sentences like: The sun glows yellow; the dog runs into the street; our old computer dies when new models are ready for purchase. Sun, dog, computer—common and clear subjects in our immediate experience. But what about God? Answer that question properly and you have all good Christian theology off and running properly. Exactly who is God?

We spoke earlier of the deadly duo that is actually the perfect pair (theology and grammar). Now we are in the center of the Christian faith and are ready to encounter a tantalizing triplet, the three-one God. We are faced with and privileged to know the divine Trinity who is an amazing Tri-Unity. Were you a math major? No matter. I assure you that this is not trick math, the joke of some old theologians, but the best way to approach an adequate understanding of the God who is revealed to us in the Bible. "Triune" is not an unnecessary complication of the truth about God's identity. It is the best (plainest) way to hold together a series of interlocking truths about the one and only God.

Who is the *Theo* of "theology"? The Apostles' Creed is organized around this Tri-Unity. The three-ness of this one-ness is the central substance of Christian theology. This chapter will focus on the first two aspects of this three-ness, who God is *eternally* and what God has done *historically* (two core theological nouns). The next chapter will complete the trio in a more verb-oriented mode by addressing what the God who is and who has acted is *now doing*—and what we should be doing in response. Theology, when whole, is oriented to the past, present, and future, and it is always God originated and God centered.

The Supreme Subject

A Christian theologian was named "Man of the Millennium" in the year 2000—imagine that, a Christian theologian being judged the most influential human to live in the last 1,000 years! Martin Luther had an obsession with God—God experienced as both present and absent, very near and sometimes too far, of wrath and of love, seemingly weak and yet certainly almighty, real and yet maybe an illusion, hidden and revealed.

Christian faith—and maybe the creation in general—begins with consideration of the God whose nature is a mystery, an amazement, an enigma, the joy above all joys, the base of believing. It centers in the coming of Jesus who enables a proper focus on the reality of God's true nature and intentions. God has Self-revealed, especially in the person of Jesus of Nazareth. Christian faith is based on the assumption that God is the eternally existing and creating One who has chosen to act redemptively in this world. The apex of God's acting is the event of Jesus Christ.

There they are, the essential nouns—the existing One, the acting One, the event of the Son through whom the acting Father has most fully expressed himself. Understanding this God and communicating well our understanding are the two critical tasks of Christian theology. Unfortunately, these tasks often are done poorly. Here's a sad example.

In late 2013 I heard a prominent leader of American Buddhists being interviewed on National Public Radio. Something he said stopped me cold, nearly made me cry. He was asked, "What about Christianity?" He responded almost sorrowfully. He had been around Christianity when a kid and had been attracted to the sweetness and forgiving and affirming spirit of Jesus. But then he had heard that behind Jesus was a Father God who was unbelievably abusive, who all along had an ugly plan to sacrifice his own boy in the worst way possible. The now-Buddhist man said, "Naturally I wanted nothing to do with that God!" Naturally.

That old cross on a hill outside ancient Jerusalem—is it an ugly symbol of an angry, wrathful, and abusive God or the ultimate hope provided by a loving and Self-sacrificing Father very worthy of our love and worship? This is the big question of theology, and little words make a big difference. Does the truth lie in understanding God *as* loving grace or *against* loving grace?

The related questions come flying. Is God *opposed* to us sinners or *open* to us sinners? Is God abusive (bad news) or redemptive (great news)? My answer is simple enough, and I am sure thoroughly biblical. It is captured in my earlier book on Christian theology that I organized around the three aspects of the Trinity God and titled *God As Loving Grace*. Don't miss the significance of the "as." God is known to us *as* the loving-grace tri-unity. . .

> *Sovereign*, the God who stands and creates, the source of loving grace;

> *Saviour*, the God who stoops and saves, the Christ initiative of loving grace;

> *Spirit*, the God who stays and sustains, the presence of loving grace.

Did you get all that? These three are really one, and the One (God) is really loving grace in eternal nature and earthly purpose. God, as known in Jesus Christ, is the supreme Subject of every proper theological sentence to be framed by Christians.

One God for All People

There are really three fundamental Christian nouns, one *God* known best in *Jesus Christ* by way of the *Bible* (which is read best with the assistance of the Spirit of the Christ). God is the base, Christ the supreme expression, and the Bible the essential medium of conveying the proper understanding of this expression. Through the Bible, set freshly aglow by the Spirit, we come to know Jesus Christ in whom is found the eternal God who is actively and savingly with us.

The General Assembly is the most representative voice of the Church of God movement (Anderson)—my particular Christian fellowship. In order to avoid more denominational division, it has refused to establish creedal statements as such. Instead, it has expressed itself on only two matters considered essential for being a Christian, two required nouns ("reformation principles") without which the heart of the faith is not present. They appear in the movement's slogan, "The Bible is our rule of faith and Christ alone is Lord."

I once wrote a book titled *Discerning the Divine*. It details the complex history of Christians searching over the centuries for an adequate understanding of God and how to express that understanding best in constantly shifting cultures. Now I want to put the matter as simply as possible. We search the sacred biblical text to learn about the Christ, who is actually God with us. We search for and find the Christ, in whom we find the true God and our own true selves and world mission. That's doing Christian theology in the plainest of language—searching, finding, focusing, and forthtelling.

You've noticed, of course, that in this book I play a little with numbers. To keep things simple, at least I have kept the numbers very small. I first introduced a deadly duo, the really perfect pair. Then I doubled the duet and came up with a quality quartet, throwing in a little geometry and calling it a quadrilateral. Then came a tantalizing triplet, a necessary three who is actually only one (God). Now, if you don't mind, I'll return to four because there is another quartet that is very important. It has to do with the one God who is for all people.

Let me approach this new quartet by introducing the metaphor of *flowing water*. Christian truth has one source of life-giving water, God. As we learn in the extended Bible story, this divine fountain gushes forth in four streams of eternal truth. Doing Christian theology well is knowing the single source and tracking the four streams, recognizing that they all carry the same water, just in four different channels, all headed lovingly our way.

Recall that Jesus once said something very telling about this amazing water and himself: "...those who drink of the water that I will give them will never be thirsty. The water that I will give will become in them a spring of water gushing up to eternal life" (John 4:14). He also said to Thomas, "I *am* the way, and the truth, and the life" (John 14:6)—in other words, the flowing of the very life of the divine to your very life and mine!

In another of my books, this one titled titled *Beneath the Surface*, I showed at length how the four truth streams of this living water flow just beneath the surface of the entire Old Testament text. Then they burst onto the surface of the New Testament in clear view, appearing in Jesus with the Bible's most careful refinement of their meaning. They join to form one truth about the life-giving God who has chosen to be *with* us and lovingly *for* us. This four-pronged truth about the ministry of the three-one God requires careful use of the earlier quartet (quadrilateral) to understand, interpret, and employ properly (that's doing theology).

Christian theology begins with the Old Testament and then flows richly and fully-watered into the New and beyond. We who follow Jesus Christ must learn from Hebrew theology. This learning focuses on fundamental Hebrew beliefs, sturdy faith nouns that also underlie the Christian faith. Here they are in brief:

1. The supreme God is, loves, and has provided a gracious word to a select people.

2. Hearers of that word of gracious selection come to know themselves to be chosen as God's treasure for a mission to live in God's way

(holiness) and for God's purposes, not for their own. God, in part through them, is ministering on behalf of all people.

3. The journey of faith and faithfulness in this fallen world will not always be easy. Even though many difficult questions may remain unanswered, God's ordering of things is fundamental and questions directed at God, even critical and doubting ones, are acceptable to God.

4. Hope in God's purposes should persist until God's fulfillment finally comes—and it will come.

The Four Truth Streams

Christians believe that in Jesus the fulfillment of God's saving purposes already has begun. Meanwhile, prior to the final fulfillment and as one means of its coming, Christian theology works to identify clearly, activate presently, and proclaim broadly the four truth streams. Here they are in brief, the basic building blocks of any adequate Christian theology.

The Eternal Fountain

One GOD for All People

| Stream #1 | Stream #2 | Stream #3 | Stream #4 |
| Covenant | Holiness | Order | Hope |

Truth Stream #1, the Way of Covenant. God has acted to choose a people with a special mission in the world. God's choice is made out of love, not because any are deserving of those being chosen. In an important sense the choice is of *all people*, with a particular people responsible for spearheading the reaching of all others. God partners with unworthy people who are made responsible for the most worthy of all purposes. The early choice was Israel and now, through Jesus, it is the body of Christ that we call the church.

Truth Stream #2, the Way of Holiness. All life is intended to be holy and pure in light of the holiness of the God who created and sustains all life. God has called a people who are to separate from this floundering world and reflect the divine life among themselves and before others. Belonging to God's people should lead to a reflecting of God's life and are engaging in God's world mission. The chosen are to be changed, "sanctified." God is prepared to transform into his own likeness those unworthy people with whom he partners.

Truth Stream #3, the Way of Ordering and Questioning. There is order and purpose in this world that originates in the creation itself. Life at its best is life lived in accord with God's created order and intended purpose. However, God has given us humans freedom of choice, and we have used it badly. The natural order of things is now disrupted and sometimes virtually invisible. The life of faith will involve questioning and searching and sometimes doubting, but nothing need lead to despair. God receives the questions and doubts of his people. God's people will always remain only partially transformed and only understand only in partially.

Truth Stream #4, the Way of Radical Hope. God enables a radical hope that can sustain faithful believers in the face of the most difficult circumstances. This hope transcends the present time with its fragile institutions and practices that too often seek to maintain the status quo in opposition to God's will and way. One day God's Messiah will come! Those in covenant with God (truth stream #1), those still in the process of being purified by God (truth stream #2), will have a persistent hope in the midst of their frustrations and unfaithfulness (truth stream #3). The fullness of the biblical story reports that the Messiah now *has come* (Jesus) and one day *will come again* to conclude the history of this time-space world and set all things right. Meanwhile, God's people are to live from the vision and stand firm in the hope it brings.

These truth streams comprise the heart of the biblical story and the basics of Christian belief. All are drawn directly from the story of Israel, especially as it finally focused in the person of Jesus. This four-fold flowing of life-giving water from the fountain of God—as highlighted by the Hebrew heritage and fulfilled in the life, death, and resurrection of Jesus—must be thought through, experienced personally, expressed wisely, and acted on in context (the quadrilateral of biblical revelation, as interpreted by reason, experience, and tradition). To engage this quad is to be doing Christian theology. To short-circuit this quad inevitably leads to a misunderstanding of God's word to us and to disappointing God with our poor theology and failed mission.

Good theology involves seeing, wading into, and being immersed in the one water source. It then involves carefully and joyfully following the four water streams that flow from the gracious divine fountain. There is only one God and one truth, but our comprehension of God, always limited, flows our way in multiple streams. They match the complexity of who we are (body, mind, and spirit), where we are (our cultural and sinful settings), and how we understand (reason, tradition, and experience).

We theologians—you and me--must keep appropriately humble, recognizing that our theological knowledge always involves *paths* of truth more than *propositions* of truth. Streams are alive and move; motionless pools tend to stagnate. Theological creeds that get fixed into final and mandatory creeds have a way of going bad. As the ancient Jews had it, and we modern Christians should have it, the Judeo-Christian faith comes to us in story form. We learn from this story how God works in our history and we come to know God's heart and intentions and our place in it all. Such story reading and telling remains a living process, the process of doing theology.

God--*As* Loving Grace

We travel our theological roads by faith and must allow the four truth streams to wash over us and carry us along. Rabbi Yeshua, Jesus the Messiah, points us directly to the fountainhead from whom all truth streams flow. "Hear, O Israel: The Lord is our God, the Lord alone" (Deut. 6:4). From God, the eternal water source, come the four streams that show us how to believe and live—and offer us the possibility of actually doing so. However, the focus, the Supreme Noun, is always to be God, the God who has spoken and is speaking. The problem is our persistent inattention to this divine communication.

A church bulletin read: The sermon of the morning is "Jesus Walks on the Water." The sermon tonight will be "Searching for Jesus." Which is it? Is Jesus the God miraculously right in front of us or the God who sadly has disappeared from us, having sunk into the deep water? We think we know him, and then we don't. He's right here, and then nowhere.

Even if we have difficulty keeping all of this straight in our church bulletins and in other communications to each other and to the public, there is no question about one thing. Jesus is the heart of Christian theology. Through Jesus we come to know God best. God is *loving grace*. The heart of the Eternal One beats for us even though we are so undeserving. "Hear this!" said Jesus. As he hung on the cross, he was saying, "See this!" The Word coming from God's mouth became flesh on our human scene (John 1:14). This becoming flesh for us—incarnation—is the keynote and centerpiece of Christianity.

The church has confessed over the centuries that Jesus *is* the eternal Word, not merely a teacher with a wise word to share. Jesus, the teacher of the word, is the Word. Jesus is the promised Messiah of the God's kingdom, not simply one who preached about it. Jesus, the preacher about the Kingdom life, is the very essence of this new life. Jesus is the eternal Savior. He is the one who heals what is wrong at the center both of our being and world history. He is not merely another healer of physical infirmities, but the Savior who takes away the sin of the whole world.

St. Paul once wrote about the divine brightness that shines in our hearts "to give us the light of the knowledge of the glory of God in the face of Christ" (2 Cor. 4:6). A redeeming glory, a loving-grace glory, suddenly had been seen in the resurrected Jesus and had captured Paul. It gave him a richer knowledge of God and a deeper experience with God than he had found as a student of Torah and in his life as a rabbi. The center of the Christian faith is the teaching that Jesus came to help us know God and be transformed back to God's likeness. God came to be like us so that we might come to be like him.

Let's return to our use of grammar. A pronoun is a word that substitutes for a noun. So we might say that Jesus is the supreme Pronoun referring back to God the Father—who is the Noun of all nouns. One is a representation, the mirror image, of the other. Said Jesus, "The Father and I are one" (John 10:30). Being alpha and omega (Rev. 1:8), Jesus is the first word to be said and the last word needing said about the truth of all times, including the very nature and purposes of God. Let's test this by reference to the world's skies as we know them.

What does the sky above Hawaii have to do with Christian theology? Nothing, except maybe one thing. Hawaii is a rare place on the planet. From there, on occasion, one can see both the North Star and the Southern Cross, the celestial icons of the two hemispheres. This unusual fact is theologically significant. It is a paradox realized in its entirety and without conflict. North Americans will recall the Civil War and Abraham Lincoln insisting in his second inaugural address that the future not be North or South, but one nation as a whole. The paradox calls for neither A nor Z, but the whole alphabet. Similarly, many basic Christian teachings are paradoxical; failing to embrace the whole of a teaching is to pervert the whole.

To repeat one of my book titles, we are "caught between truths" or we are wrong. Was Jesus truly a human being? Yes. Was Jesus truly God with us? Yes. Is he the North Star or the Southern Cross? Yes. According to standard (orthodox) and paradoxical Christian belief, God is both sovereign and omnipresent—big theological words. God is way out there and also everywhere that we are or can ever be. Put differently, the *high* of God became clearer to us humans when the *nigh* of God breeched the divine-human gap by coming to us *in person*, coming as the Almighty one in the form of a servant Son. The Creator becomes known to us best in a cradle! The Almighty is seen best in a helpless baby, and without being any less almighty in the process. Can you handle a paradox like that?

This line of truth begins to speak to the concern of our American Buddhist friend mentioned earlier. Being attracted to Jesus actually is coming to know God. Paul speaks in the New Testament against a common and awful misconception. Jesus did *not* die in order to change his Father's mind about us sinners. It is *not* true that God could—would—forgive us *only* if he was paid a big enough ransom to satisfy his honor deeply wounded by our sin. It is *not* the terrible case that only with a dead Son does the Father become the lover and healer of wayward children. No! The coming, life, death, and resurrection of Jesus is proof of God's eternal love, a *demonstration* of and not a *changing* of God's heart. Jesus did not come to change God's mind but to show it dramatically before the whole world.

Alleluia is a classic work in the world of Christian music. First released in 1973, it was created by my treasured friends Bill and Gloria Gaither. In 2013, on its fortieth anniversary, my wife and I were privileged to sing in a mass choir presenting this work again with full orchestra on the campus of Anderson University. What's so special about this music? It's about the center of Christian faith, Jesus. Songs in this powerful presentation include "There's Something About that Name," "King of Kings—Lord of Lords," and "Because He Lives."

Interspersed among the songs are testimonies, ancient and modern, of people who contacted Jesus and were loved into new life by the sheer grace and redeeming love of God seen in him. Tax collectors, fisherman, prostitutes, and politicians came to agree that there's just something very different about Jesus—and thus about God. And since Jesus lives and loves, so can they—and we! At one point the narration of *Alleluia* goes like this:

> If Christ had been a philosopher
>   they could have debated Him.
> If He had been a warrior
>   they could have fought Him.
> Had he been a religionist
>   they could have ignored Him as an eccentric.
> But Christ was love...
>   and what do you do with that?

What do you do? That certainly is the key question.

Here's my answer. You bow in gratitude and rise in newness of life! These actions are the follow-throughs that constitute the process of doing Christian theology. The first actions are the identifying and embracing of the core nouns of the faith—God, Christ, Bible. Then come the verbs, the resulting new beings and related actions that are based on and empowered by the basic nouns. If God is, and is like Jesus Christ, then who are we *to be* and what are we *to do*? The essential nouns lead to the essential verbs.

12

THE ESSENTIAL VERBS

Question: How much real spiritual life infuses your statements of belief? What doesn't pulse and move and make a difference is hardly alive and true in the fullest sense. All good sentences move from stable nouns to active verbs.

We've now looked at the noun side of theological things. On this more fixed side, we have realized that there are fewer essential and stable nouns, ones that should be believed absolutely, than most believers think. We now come to the more active arena of the faith. Beyond what we believe mentally lies this big theological question. What should we be *becoming* and *doing* because of what we believe? This is the verb side of theological things. The fullness of good theology goes beyond the "whats" to the "so whats" and "hows." It moves from the fixed nouns to the flowing verbs of true believing.

Believing, Being, Doing

Here is Christian belief put as briefly as possible. We believe in the God who was in Jesus Christ for our salvation. Believing this naturally leads us in a particular direction. We are led to attitudes and actions consistent with and mandated by this salvation message. We are challenged to be *changed* and *act* on the essential nouns, to bring personal attitudes and actions in line with the implications of God in Christ for us. Our Christian witness to the world will be judged primarily by who we *are* and what we *do*, not merely by what words we use for the subjects of our believing. Beyond the right words that express commitment to the right things, good theology involves actually living the right life.

How do we do this, live a life consistent with the right words—words about God and the four truth streams that flow from the divine fountain-heart of loving grace? It's very challenging indeed since it will demand your all. The goal is straightforward. Once the true God is properly understood from the biblical revelation of Jesus Christ, the life actions of believers are to reflect who God is and how God acts. It's that simple—and demanding.

Christians are to embrace the nouns central to biblical revelation—and then do more. We are to "have the same mind in you that was in Christ Jesus" (Philippians 2:5). This Christ mind involves an emptying, a humility, and "even death on a cross" (2:6-8). No wonder many believers prefer to stay with the right words and not get too involved with their big life implications.

Let's put this another way. The Spirit of God is none other than God now present and active among us. Therefore, we who believe are to be acting in line with how the Spirit is acting. Theology, having clarified the nature of the true God, goes on to an understanding of how God has and is acting (the natural overflow of God's nature). Once we understand that, we can know how to be acting ourselves. As I wrote some years ago, we must find "the way beyond dead orthodoxy [being stuck on only the nouns of the faith] to the authentic Christian faith of the heart, a faith that is both text anchored [biblical] and Spirit enlivened."[42]

Life in the Spirit has to do with internalizing and implementing the good news that has come in Jesus. It calls for human stories to be changed by exposure to the biblical story of God in Christ. Christian life is the life of God mediated through Jesus Christ to believers through the power and ministry of the Spirit of God. Believers are to affirm Jesus as truth's norm and life guide. The Spirit of Jesus is the *ruach* of God, the *pneuma* of God, the divine breath, wind, living power that (who) creates, liberates, enables people to anticipate and represent the coming and already present reign of God.

The Spirit enabling involves both the *fruit* and *gifts* of the Spirit to believers. The fruit (Gal. 5:22-23) are the privilege of all believers. They are the natural reflections and expressions of the life of the Spirit who has come to dwell within and seeks to flow outward into all dimensions of life. The gifts are given selectively as God chooses (1 Cor. 12:11), with all believers receiving one or more. They are given as needed for the fulfillment of the church's life and mission (Eph. 4:11-12). We are to believe rightly (the core nouns of the faith) and live accordingly (the core verbs of the faith). We are to live producing Spirit fruit and using Spirit gifts.

Seven Essential Verbs

Nouns are good. They are the necessary theological subjects, the fixed realities, the foundations of the faith. But they are only the base and the beginning. Noun-subjects must *become* in us and *do* through us things appropriate to what they are. They must lead to verb-beings and verb-doings. The grammatical logic of Christian theology runs as follows. If *this* is the case, then I must *become* this and *do* this. Notice my stressing the "I"? If it doesn't get personal, your intellectual believing will never add up to much.

I give a full-chapter treatment to each of seven essential truth verbs in my book *Authentic Spirituality*. Following here—staying faithful to my goal of keeping things short and simple—is the heart of each of these verbs of Christian *being* and *doing*. Because God *is* the eternal Subject, and because God is eternally *like Jesus*, his Self-revealing Son, then the Bible unveils the basic Spirit-oriented verbs of Christian life. They are:

> I (you) must—*see* the open and reaching God
> I (you) must—*experience* this God calling me
> I (you) must—*be amazed* at God's gracious extravagance
> I (you) must—*come to know* with the Spirit's help
> I (you) must—*learn to live* by the Spirit's power
> I (you) must—*walk* the path of sanctification
> I (you) must—*accept* the Spirit's assurance and thus abide

I will introduce one special word to help make each one of these central life-verbs clear. One word each sounds easy, I know, but there will be a slight complication—not more than you can handle. The word will be from the ancient Greek language. I also will use a little poetry related to each.

Poetry is a very verb-like kind of communication. It's truth in motion, the dancing of a delicate picture more than the standing of a staid sentence. It's the going beyond your brain to the rhythms of your body and the emotions of your heart. So, here we go—essential verbs, important words, bits of poetry, all the building blocks of foundational Christian theology. They highlight the motion stimulated by the ministry of the Spirit who flows through the biblical truth streams and right into and then through our lives of faith.

1. I must—*see* the open and reaching God. No Christian teaching is more central than the nature of God. How we understand God deeply affects our understanding of creation, the incarnation of God in Jesus, divine grace, election, and sovereignty, human salvation, prayer, suffering and the future. We spoke earlier of God as the supreme noun of Christian theology. Now we note that the first verb in the Chrstian's theological sentence is "to see" this God properly.

Here's our first special word—*epiginosko*. The Greek *ginosko* means to know. When you put the prefix *epi* in front of it, it gets intensified into really knowing. That's what we want, to truly perceive, to know intimately, not just intellectually but in a way that alters life itself. The two men on their way to Emmaus saw the resurrected Jesus and had a casual conversation with him. It was all surface awareness, a mere chat with a stranger. Then over a meal at home "their eyes were opened, and they recognized him" (Luke 24:31). Finally, they knew who he was! They moved from knowing to *really* knowing, from *ginosko* to *epiginosko*.

A good place to gain biblical understanding of God is by recalling a parable told by Jesus. God is pictured as a father longing for a loving relationship with his two sons (Luke 15:11-32). This parable is more about the father (God) and less about the "prodigal son. Who is God when we really see him in depth and in relation to our human waywardness? It comes to involve a forgiving and restoring father throwing a party!

God is a loving "person" seeking freely-chosen relationships of love with his creatures. God is not an all-controlling despot who tolerates no resistance. To the contrary, "God's fair beauty according to Scripture is his own relationality as a triune community. It is God's gracious interactivity, not his hyper-transcendence and/or immobility, which makes him so glorious."[43] God comes close, becomes vulnerable to our callous waywardness, and expresses a wonderful mercy in spite of it all. God is transcendent, very high, and also immanent, coming right to us where we are. The coming is nothing short of amazing love.

The fundamental Christian belief is reported in Colossians 1:15-23. Not only does God exist, but we sinful humans have been visited and touched by the divine. In Christ Jesus, all was created, and in Christ Jesus all things now hold together. The biblical picture of God as the almighty and creating Father emphasizes with the power of almightiness a loving grace. God acts in accord with the loving nature of a merciful Father. Such graceful acting is wholly undeserved by us. It reaches out and is open to us despite everything. God risks on our behalf and is available for real relationships. We must really see this amazing truth and allow it overwhelm who we are and how we view and act toward everything else.

A gracious interweaving of prayer and Scripture opens the door to in-depth awareness of God. Only then are we ready for God to clothe us in love, wonder, and wisdom. As expressed in the hymn lyrics by Clara H. Scott, the natural prayer of a Christian is:

> Open my eyes that I may see
> Glimpses of truth Thou hast for me;
> Place in my hands the wonderful key,
> That shall unclasp and set me free.

2. I must—*experience* God calling *me*. The openness of God is expressed in an active and redemptive reaching toward us sinful humans. We are being summoned from on high—and not just we, but *me*! The Spirit of God is truly present with us even though we are so undeserving. This presence, however, is not meaningful to us unless we actually experience it and respond. Prophets of ancient Israel and many more contemporary Christian leaders have challenged the faith communities they knew. They have scolded believers for being stale pools of mere religion, robots and pawns of a non-experiencing and non-responding traditionalism. Such people may have been right on paper but very wrong in practice.

Theology must be more than an arid doctrinal formulations and a mindless repetition of traditional words. Authentic Christianity involves hearing God's call to us individually. It invites a realizing of the divine presence in our own depths and a responding to God's reaching love by loving others as we have been loved. Good theology is not merely organizing and agreeing with some good thoughts about God, even ones that are totally true to biblical revelation. It also is the living response of our entire selves to the revealed fact of Jesus Christ now with us in the life of the Spirit.

We must be changed in our right beliefs into God's likeness by experiencing our own life-change, the intended impact of God's calling to us and presence with us. The church is to be the gathering of people who are alive in Christ and full of the fruit of the Spirit. Its members are the people who have realized that God is reaching toward them lovingly. The church's true members are the people who have opened themselves to experience all that this gracious reaching can and should mean.

Let me share a personal testimony that is a moving poetry singing into God's ears. It's the classic report of John Wesley about his own in-depth spiritual awakening.

> On May 24, 1738, I went very unwillingly to a society in Aldersgate Street [London], where one was reading Luther's preface to the Epistle to the Romans. About a quarter before nine, while he was thus describing the changes which God works in the heart through faith in Christ, I felt my heart *strangely warmed*; I felt I did trust in Christ, Christ alone for salvation; and an assurance was given me that he had taken away my sins, *even mine*, and saved me from the law of sin and death.[44]

The truth was always in the book. Suddenly, however, its warmth had flooded into a tender heart, and that personal intimacy is what made all the difference!

What about the special Greek word? It is *parakletos*. The *kletos* part is the calling of God to each of us. But when it is intensified with the prefix *para*, then we have the God who is calling and also coming personally *to our very sides* as a healing and guiding companion. The God who calls has now called *me*.

In the Gospel of John the "Paraclete" is the word for the Holy Spirit. This Spirit is the Comforter calling to us and coming to us. God's calling is no distant communication from far out in the blue; it's a still small voice echoing in our very insides. The creating God the Father and the redeeming God the Son are well beyond us and yet truly available to be *in* and *through* us (the immediately present and actively ministering God the Spirit). The biblical story of God-with-us moves from the event of the risen Christ to the ongoing reality of the ever-present Spirit of the Christ. I *truly see* and I *actually experience*.

3. I must—*be amazed* at God's gracious extravagance. Are you prepared to really see and experience God as both the ultimate One and the One who is vulnerably Self-giving, God as far beyond and yet deep within? This is hard to get one's mind around, almost too amazing to be true. However, if the reality and mystery of God were simple enough to be fully comprehended by us humans, God would neither be great enough to be worshipped nor wonder-full enough to be adored. When we finite humans approach the infinite God, we must be overcome with a sense of awe and astonishment.

When our best understanding of God is found in a vulnerable baby born in a barn in Bethlehem and then hanging on a cross outside Jerusalem, we must temper our concept of the "all-powerful" One with the revealed reality of the "all-loving" One. The faith of Christians began when a shocked and scattered band of depressed disciples got news that was just too good to be true. Their beloved Jesus had been cruelly killed. Hope had been dashed. Faith apparently had been folly. But wait? He is risen! Jesus had conquered death. The power of death had itself died. God was still with us in this ever-living Christ. Amazing!

Our Greek word? It's *hyperbole* which has come directly into English as hyperbole, an obvious exaggeration, something bigger than real life. How about this as an example? "I just ate a mile-high ice cream cone!" The truth? It was a really big one, but not literally a mile of piled-up calories. We use exaggeration as a way of expressing the wonder of something really good. Something truly amazing should happen in the world of Christian theology. There comes the daring announcement that there are a few things too good to be literally true, and yet they actually *are true*!

A very few things are so good that even our apparent exaggerations are not big enough to reach the fullness of their actual reality. In Ephesians 1:15-23 Paul reports that we humans have been confronted with things so outrageously wonderful that it is difficult to put them into human language. The divine love, grace, and power resident in Jesus Christ reach well beyond all other events, persons, and truth claims ever encountered by humanity.[45] Read these verses and truly marvel.

God has bridged the gap between himself and us, restored the relationship possibility, and given fallen humans the undeserved grace needed to realize this marvelous reconciliation. God risks our human responses, drawing by love rather than manipulating by a carefully calculated providence. God is an awesomely loving and grace-giving God! God is love and those who abide in God intentionally abide in a reciprocal love relationship with God and then with each other (1 John 4:16-18). The Christian life should be a trail of amazement and an adventure in adoration. At the heart of Christian theology is this extravagant message expressed well by Annie Johnson Flint:

> God's love has no limit,
> His grace has no measure,
> His power has no boundary known unto men;
> For out of his infinite riches in Jesus,
> He giveth and giveth and giveth again!

4. I must—come to *know* with the Spirit's help. Seeing, experiencing, and being amazed begins to add up to true knowledge of God, the kind that changes lives and worlds. Knowing the God who is beyond the reach of our full comprehension is the possible impossibility of our Christian faith journey. Paul prays that Christians might "know the love of Christ that surpasses knowledge, so that [we] may be filled with all the fullness of God" (Eph. 3:19)—actually knowing what surpasses knowledge!

The goal of such grace-enabled faith knowing is not gaining an impressive library of religious information. Instead, we seek relationship with the Fountain of knowledge so that we "may know you, the only true God, and Jesus Christ whom you have sent" (John 17:3). From this one truth Fountain (as we explained above) there flows four streams of truth. To "know" in matters of the faith is intimately related to knowing the Knower of all things (God), and allowing the truth streams to flow into and through us as the living water of the Spirit. Sheep can do without answers to many questions. What they cannot do without is knowing and being close to their shepherd. The Lord Jesus is our Shepherd (Psalm 23).

The key? Knowledge of God comes primarily through God's Self-revelation. And where is that found? It is in Jesus Christ as he becomes known in the biblical story. And how is the Bible story best understood? It is understood in depth only through the present ministry of God's Spirit *within us*. Knowledge of God is not mere "experience," how I "feel" about things. Nonetheless, it is a byproduct of the Spirit's intimate work within. We should "pray the Bible" by reading in expectant reverence and experiencing the testimony of the prophet Jeremiah as he once addressed God: "Your words were found, and I ate them, and your words became to me a joy and the delight of my heart" (Jer. 15:16).

Ate them? Ingest the revelation of God? Yes, we are to "taste and see that the Lord is good" (Psalm 34:8). We must remove the obstructions between head and heart so that reading the Bible can lead to the kind of intimate understanding that is life transforming. We must both *analyze* the sacred words and *ingest* them. Head and heart must work as a team.

We don't need another Greek word here—*gnosis* still works fine. Said Jesus, "If you continue in my word, you are truly my disciples; and you will *know* the truth, and the truth will make you free" (Jn. 8:31-32). We will see (know) well—and be free--only when we are looking through the eyes of the Spirit. The Bible is best understood by the present *illumination* of the Spirit who long ago *inspired* its original composition.

We know so little, really, but God's Spirit leads us to necessary knowledge in the midst of all our unknowing. Here are a few poetic lines of Daniel W. Whittle that share true confidence in the midst of great humility:

I know not why God's wondrous grace, To me He hath made known,
Nor why, unworthy, Christ in love, Redeemed me for His own....

I know not how this saving faith, To me He did impart,
Nor how believing in His word, Wrought peace within my heart....

I know not how the Spirit moves, Convincing men of sin....
I know not when my Lord may come, At night or noonday fair,
Nor if I'll walk the vale with Him, Or meet Him in the air.

But I know whom I have believed, and am persuaded that He is able
To keep that which I've committed, Unto Him against that day.

We know so little, very little for sure, and yet we possess all the knowing we need concerning what is essential. Thanks be to God!

5. I must—learn to *live* by the Spirit's power. Christian spiritual life is particularly concerned with the joining of theology and practical life in the church and world. The concern is not to live in *our* way, but in the way *of the Spirit*. No creedalism or ceremonialism alone will ever meet God's requirement for the good life (Isa. 1:11-17; Amos 5:21-25). Those who please God are those who *act justly* and *love mercy* and *walk humbly* with God (Micah 6:8). Much of what we come to know involves how we are *to live*.

Do you get those essential Christian verbs that must be in all good theological sentences? Act...love...walk. For the ancient Hebrews and contemporary Christians—you and me, "truth was not so much an idea to be contemplated as an experience to be lived, a deed to be done."[46] What we *think* theologically must also be what we *do* in everyday life. To think rightly and yet live wrongly is to eliminate the rightness, even if we can word it perfectly. Theology involves the wholeness of thinking, being, and doing.

Said Jesus: "And everyone who hears these words of mine and does not *act on them* will be like a foolish man who built his house on sand. The rain fell, and the floods came, and the winds blew and beat against that house, and it fell—and great was its fall!" (Matt. 7:26-27). John reports that anyone claiming to know Jesus well and yet does not follow his commands is obviously a liar (I John 2:4). We must walk our talk, live our theology.

Ready for the Greek word? It's a wonderful word about authentic faith that shows itself in Christ-like living. The word is *kosmeo*, meaning to adorn or make more attractive (transferred to English as "cosmetic"). A Christian must become a credit to the cause of Christ by adorning Christian teaching with the Christ-quality of actual new life. We are to be "an ornament to the doctrine of God our Savior" (Titus 2:10). Once a woman or man embraces the Christian verbs of seeing, experiencing, and being amazed, that believer is to become an effective, infectious, winsome, and honorable representative of the King of kings and Lord of lords. To use Paul's daring words, "it is no longer I who live, but it is Christ who lives in [and through] me" (Gal. 2:20).

God is not an abstract concept for the library shelf or a mere philosophy of life for elite intellectuals. God is the Eternal Person, the very present One who has become involved with us humans, visibly, understandably, because in the person Jesus (Col. 1:15). Since God has chosen "incarnation," being enfleshed here with us, we must do much the same, enfleshing in ourselves and thus visibly living out our faith in the world around us. The biblical tradition makes no distinction between the "sacred" and the "secular" arenas of life. All life is a unity. It's all God's domain; it's our place of ministry and mission.

Got that? Everything is theological! The results of our believing are intended to envelop the whole of our persons and impact the whole of our communities. The New Testament does not present a unified systematic theology, but it does tell a unified story. This story centers in the actions of God, especially in Israel and then in Jesus. The plot unfolds toward the creation by creating a community of witnesses to the good news of God's redeeming love.

God's love must *define* and then *radiate from* the children of God in Christ. Theology involves both the defining and radiating—two critical verbs of Christian theology and life.

Instead of a systematic theology, what the New Testament does present are root metaphors or essential verbs that should define the Christian life. They are:

1. ...*being* an alternative model of life witness to the world—church;
2. ...*living* the way of Jesus through the church's life—cross;
3. ...*exhibiting* the firstfruits of the coming of God's future—new creation.[47]

Good theology necessarily includes the verbs of being, living, and exhibiting. Said Martin Luther King, Jr.: "Don't ever let anyone pull you so low as to hate them. We must use the weapon of love. We must have compassion and understanding for those who hate us.... We stand in life at midnight; we are always on the threshold of a new dawn."[48]

Quality living is accepting the apology that has not yet been offered. Jesus adorned even his dying by his Father-like forgiveness of those who were killing him (Luke 23:34). To be Christ's is to have in us this same attitude toward even our enemies (Matt. 5:44). It must be active and visible. Here are its important marks as put in the hymn lyrics of Charles W. Naylor:

> Are you adorning the doctrine, The glorious doctrine of God,
> Walking so holy before Him, Following where He has trod,
> So when the world looks upon you, Nothing but Christ is in view?
> So when the world looks upon you, Nothing but Christ is in view?

6. I must—*walk* the path of sanctification. To be spiritual in the Christian sense is to be so aware of Jesus and so influenced by his Spirit that all aspects of life become *Spirit-shaped* and *Spirit-directed*. This is what it means to be "sanctified," hidden in Christ with God and having the same mind as did Jesus because of the Spirit's life within. We become "holy" only by being filled with a radical amazement about the greatness and graciousness of God and then being changed increasingly to reflect that likeness (2 Cor. 3:18). To be holy like this is hard—but it's where true theology and true life are found and become infectious.

The holy life is a an undeserved gift, and yet it is not sustained without disciplined effort—another of those critical paradoxes. Believers need to exercise means of spiritual growth, some of which are especially established by God for this purpose. But all such means for growth have a major limitation. They are not magical—no one goes through the right motions with the automatic result of gaining a matured holiness. The methods of gaining spiritual growth are crucial, God-given, but worthless apart from proper motivation for their use and the present ministry of the Spirit of God. The motions of God-likeness lack value without the breath of God enlivening them in us. To play-act godliness is a hypocrisy so evident (and disgusting) to others.

I have written a book on this very subject—*Catch Your Breath! Exhaling Death and Inhaling Life* (2014). In brief, here's how the New Testament puts it: "Therefore prepare your minds for action; discipline yourselves.... Like obedient children, do not be conformed to the desires that you formerly had in ignorance. Instead, as he who called you is holy, be holy yourselves in all your conduct" (1 Pet. 1:13-15). "Train yourself in godliness for, while physical training is of some value, godliness is valuable in every way" (1 Tim. 4:7-8).

Doing the work of theology without a growing personal holiness is only an arid intellectual exercise in trying to think properly. The larger goal is a winning witness in the world, and that depends on a believer's transformation into what C. S. Lewis once called "little Christs." We are to be transformed into the likeness of Jesus "until Christ is formed in you" (Gal. 4:19). To be "holy" is to be more than being forgiven of sin and agreeing to "orthodox" theological thoughts. It is to gain possession of Christ-like character, be filled with Christ-breath, and then *to act accordingly*. Here is where a key New Testament word comes into play.

Jesus announced that we must be "perfect" even as the Father in heaven is perfect (Matt. 5:48). *Teleioo* means to make perfect. Christians are said to be yes/no people in this regard, people *not yet* made perfect even as they now *are* perfect—another critical paradox. Paul testifies humbly, "Not that I have already obtained this or have already reached the goal, but I press on to make it my own" (Phil 3:12). And yet, "No one has ever seen God; if we love one another, God lives in us, and his love *is perfected in us*" (1 Jn. 4:12). Christian perfection means to be cooperating with God's transforming grace, fulfilling Paul's instruction to "be imitators of God, as beloved children, and *live in love*, as Christ loved us" (Eph. 5:1-2). We both *are* and one day *will be*.

To be "entirely sanctified" is more about being *full* than *complete*. A person can be full of God's love and joy and yet be incomplete, still on the way, still in the making. When we are breathing the very wind of God, we are not God, to be sure, but we truly are God's redeemed and really alive children. Here lies an important paradox. It is a recognition that there is *progression* in our *perfection,* always a going on from wherever we already are. Love is the core meaning of holiness as Jesus demonstrated it for us and expects of us, and love can be full without being static, real without being fully realized. It can be mature and still in motion. The hymn "Take Time to Be Holy" by William Longstaff and George Stebbins says it well:

> Take time to be holy, Speak often with God;
> Find rest in Him always, And feed on His Word.
> Make friends of God's children, Help those who are weak,
> Forgetting in nothing His blessing to seek.

Notice the essential verbs of Christian life—taking, speaking, finding, feeding, making, helping, and remembering.

7. I must—*accept* the Spirit's assurance and *abide*. Life in this world, even life as known by theologically correct and Spirit-active and thus holy believers, will be less than ideal. Knowledge is limited, growth incomplete, bodies fragile, friends sometimes faithless, and our best efforts not always successful. So there are two other verbs essential for our faith lives. We must *accept* and *abide*.

Following the events of Pentecost (see the Book of Acts), the vivid presence of the Spirit of Jesus heightened the expectations of the disciples, propelled them into active and daring mission, enlivened their worship, and certainly increased their preparation for the eventual re-appearance of the Lord of the harvest. The pages of the New Testament rustle with breathless reports about the resurrection of Jesus, the dramatic coming of Christ's Spirit, and what still lies in store for all who believe. Eternal life was and still is in the wind. The Spirit was awakening, inspiring, and filling with "all joy and peace in believing" so that, by the power of the Spirit, believers might *abound in hope* (Rom. 15:13). The future was assured and, at least in part, was already invading the present. What will be already is!

There is a wonderful biblical word sturdy enough to sustain believers for the roughest of roads on the journey through this life and beyond. It is *hypomeno* which means "dwelling" or "remaining." It means being safely sheltered, standing fast, being patient, living within and under the sovereignty, protection, and control of God. It is the stance of faith by grace that provides spiritual staying power.

The hope of surviving and even thriving "until then" lies in the right abiding, residing under the wings of an assurance that only the presence and power of the Spirit of God can provide. There may be no physical safety and no easy answers in this world, but there is the promise of the abiding divine presence that will outlast and finally overcome it all. To abide in the love of Christ makes one's joy complete (John 15:9-11). We can rejoice in our present sufferings because we know that they can produce a perseverance that enhances Christian character and actually enlivens Christian hope (Rom. 5:3-4).

Are you ready for a little poetry to be added to our wonderful Greek word? In the words of William O. Cushing, real safety is found only under the wings of God:

> Under His wings I am safely abiding;
> Though the night deepens and tempests are wild,
> Still I can trust Him; I know He will keep me;
> He has redeemed me, and I am His child.

And here is more assuring warmth from the great hymn "A Mighty Fortress Is Our God" by Martin Luther:

> Did we in our own strength confide,
> Our striving would be losing,
> Were not the right Man on our side,
> The Man of God's own choosing.
> Dost ask who that may be?
> Christ Jesus, it is He;
> Lord Sabaoth His name,
> From age to age the same,
> *And he must win the battle.*

13

BENCH PLAYERS

Question: Can you see how sloppy grammar makes for sloppy theology? Keep a close eye on even the smaller pieces of a sentence. Sometimes those sitting on the bench can be as important as those playing on the court or field.

In case you're not a sports fan, just know this. There always is a starting team, the frontline people. Then there are others sitting on the bench waiting their turn to get into the action when they are needed (someone graduates or gets hurt, tired, or under-performs). Sometimes it's a pinch runner adding needed flash and speed on the base-paths at a critical time. Sometimes it's a pinch batter who isn't quite good enough to start but brings power to the plate when the game is on the line. You get the general idea. A team without a good bench is usually in big trouble late in the game.

When we think about Christian theology as a sentence, with God the primary subject (actor), his redeeming grace the critical action (verb), and we sinful folks the fortunate objects, we must realize something very important. A good sentence, and good theology, usually has more than nouns, verbs, and objects. There are important bench players, especially verb tenses, adjectives, adverbs, and punctuation marks. These add color, pace, clarity, and manner to the action just when they are needed—and they usually are. Good theology uses them often and carefully.

Do you remember chapter six about the deadly duo that turns out to be the perfect pair? Theology and grammar are hardly the most popular of subjects, but they go together very well when understood properly, and they control the appropriateness of our believing and the effectiveness of our witnessing and living. We already have looked at the central nouns and verbs of Christian faith. Now we turn to the bench players. A good theological grammarian is sensitive to the bench and knows what to insert into the game—and exactly when.

Didn't Jesus say, "To be my disciples, you must go into the world and write and live great theological sentences"? I can't find the precise biblical location of this quote, but I'm sure he said it—or something close to it. Maybe it was, "teaching them to obey everything that I have commanded you" (Matt. 28:20). We are to teach the truth of who Jesus was and is and what his mission in the world was all about for him and for us now. And we are to live in such a way that we reflect him, which is the only way to make our witness authentically Christian.

Critical Punctuation Marks

I once heard a great sermon about the important punctuation marks of a mature Christian faith. There were humorous and truly sad illustrations of the misuse of the marks. Getting them right is getting Christian belief and life right. Getting them wrong can be embarrassing at best and a disaster at worst. These marks are little things in themselves, but they make a big difference when used properly.

Here are three punctuation marks that must be taken seriously when doing Christian theology. I call them theology's bench players not because they are relatively unimportant, but because they seem to be mere add-ons and don't get the press of the frontline folks. Without them, however, a team is likely to lose—and theology is likely to be badly out of balance.

1. **Exclamation Points (!).** These are rarely justified. Unfortunately, we often tend to make our personal opinions or denomination's perspectives more definitive and dramatic than they deserve.

"Women should not be real clergy in church life!" In this sentence there's a dramatic grammatical emphasis quite misplaced. Some Christians are passionate about such a restriction of leadership, but it's based on questionable biblical interpretation and is hardly consistent with how Jesus carried on his ministry. Regardless of the arguments for and against, my point is that such a restriction of leadership hardly deserves an (!)—how about a (?)? Beliefs of this kind are not even close to one of the few beliefs that are truly deserving, like "Jesus is Lord!"

2. **Commas (,).** The theological point to be made about commas is that we should be most careful not to claim that what is *ongoing* is really *finished*. You'll see this played out extensively in what I say below about verb tenses in theology. We tend to say, "It happened and is over (period)" when the thing is still something actually in process.

We are "saved" from sin by God's sheer grace (*comma* or *period*?). Because the salvation issue is never a fully done deal while we yet live in this world, a theologian should opt for the comma. Of course, God's saving work is fully done in the life, death, and resurrection of Jesus (! and .), but we sinners saved by grace are still in the salvation process (,).

3. **Question Marks (?).** The question mark suggests a level of still not knowing. Christians who capitalize on exclamation points and tend to use numerous periods where commas belong usually run scared of question marks. They insist: "We are to preach the truth, not dialogue about it as though it's up for grabs." But what's wrong with a little humility and doubt? A mature person has little fear of being self-critical, and doubt can be a valuable means of clarification. Doubt has a way of exposing false securities and even idolatrous views. To realize the helpful possibilities of honest doubt is to be freed to plunge more deeply into an honest faith.

Let's not forget that theology deals with the largest questions of human origin, identity, and destiny. Gaining perspective on all this is necessarily a matter of faith as well as knowledge. Our knowledge will always have its limitations. One can know and still not know. We must move beyond feeling guilty for sometimes doubting our faith and questioning God. Indeed, there may be more genuine faith in honest doubt than in a blind acceptance of some conventional creed that is thoughtlessly held. Bring your questions off the bench and into the game.

Segments of a Great Theological Sentence

Beyond the basics of nouns and verbs and punctuation marks, there are four more parts of good grammar that can add much to the making of a good theological sentence. They involve the *number* of actors (singular/plural), the *timing* of the action (tenses), the *manner* of the action (adverbs), and the *appearance* of the actors while they are acting (adjectives). Each is an important segment of a proper theological sentence.

1. Singular/Plural. There is the question of numbers or the limits of God's saving grace. In today's shrinking global village, the question of numbers is more pressing than ever. Who can be saved, just us, or us and them, a few or potentially everybody, only good Christians or even good folks in other faith communities? A mature believer will dare to raise this question of numbers.

Nothing is quite as simple as we would like. The truth we humans can know is singular and plural according to the Bible. Here is the singular. Jesus is the *one* way to God. He is *the* way, truth, and life, with no one coming to the Father except through him (John 14:6). There is no authentic Christian teaching that is not consistent with the revelation of God in Jesus Christ. He alone is the touchstone for truth, life, and salvation.

That's the dramatic singular. And now for the plural. God has not left himself without witness anywhere, even though God is Self-revealed definitively in the particular life, death, and resurrection of Jesus. Yes, God's Self-revelation in Jesus is of surpassing worth and the yardstick for measuring the value of supposed revelations found elsewhere. But the Bible also leads us to believe that the Spirit of the Christ is lovingly drawing all of humanity into the range of Christ's saving work, always and everywhere.

While celebrating the singularity—using an exclamation point, we must not become so arrogant as to pronounce that there is no plurality, that we alone are the chosen and privileged, the only ones in the know. The Spirit of Christ is the heart of the church, but never its prisoner. The Spirit blows freely and lovingly on all humanity. The norm that God uses to judge all persons is Jesus Christ (Rom. 2:13-16), but all people are not judged by whether or not they actually knew Jesus in the flesh or by direct witness to him. Many who never heard the Jesus name can yet be touched lovingly and savingly by who Jesus is, what he has done, and what his Spirit is now doing. Plurality says that God is God, not us. God is the grace-giver and final judge, not us. We prefer the singular; God loves the whole world.

At age 87, Billy Graham, the famous Christian evangelist, was interviewed by Jon Meacham in the log home on a mountaintop in North Carolina where Graham had lived for decades. This beloved Christian leader had been friends with ten American presidents and preached the gospel of Jesus Christ to more humans than anyone else in history. He now spoke to his interviewer about "mysteries and moderation." He announced humbly his matured "appreciation of complexity."

Then came the singular/plural issue. When asked if good Jews, Muslims, Buddhists, and Hindus would be allowed by God into heaven, Graham said quietly: "Those are decisions only the Lord will make. It would be foolish for me to speculate on who will be there and who won't.... I believe the love of God is absolute.... Salvation is the work of Almighty God, and only he knows what is in each human heart."[49] That's the cautious but open pluralism of a good theological sentence.

2. Tenses (past, present, future). Here is the question of time, the whens of our salvation. My New Testament teacher in seminary stressed that the ancient Greek language was highly sophisticated when it comes to grammar. For instance, it had eight tenses, each specifying a slightly different state of the action being carried on by the verb of a sentence. Was the action a single act, one now going on, one now finished, one finished but with continuing results, one yet to happen, etc. The variations of each tense, he insisted, were carefully chosen by the biblical writers to convey precise theological meanings. He saw theological teaching in every grammatical nuance. Whether or not he was a little overboard on this theology-everywhere thing will not be argued here. Even so, there is little question that the tense of a verb is often theologically critical.

Let me comment on the three standard tenses you would think of immediately, past, present, and future. They all are found in the wonderful New Testament word *huiothesia*. The basic noun *huio*, "son," is put into action when compounded by *thesia*, "placing," creating the composite meaning of "placing a son." This placement—adoption—appears biblically in all three tenses—past event, present process, and future prospect. Keeping these clear is theologically important.

"Salvation" is a three-tensed thing. Entrance into God's family involves understanding the present possibility and embracing the future prospect, both of which are defined by a known past event. To be adopted by God today is a glorious flash in the blazing glory of God's adoptive nature and long history and coming future with us humans. Before the foundation of the world, God "destined us for adoption as his children through Jesus Christ" (Eph. 1:3-5). Such a pivotal past provides the framework for present faith.

Given that past, the present tense of salvation (being saved) is an ongoing process. We who enter into the saving effects of the past work of God in Jesus are in the process of receiving the full rights of being God's grace-children. Even so, we have not yet received the full realities of our rich inheritance. Jesus leads and guides us along the path of a faith journey (Acts 5:31; Heb. 2:10 and 12:2). To be holy, fully saved and restored, is to really belong to Jesus and be in the active process of being formed by the Christ-like vision, practices, beliefs, and mission of the people of God.

Where are the past roots and present fruits of our salvation process headed? Paul says that "we ourselves, who have the first fruits of the Spirit, groan inwardly while we wait for adoption, the redemption of our bodies" (Rom. 8:23). God's people are to live toward the future when there will be the fullness of God's intention—love, justice, wholeness, completed salvation for his children. Living out of God's past and toward God's future makes today a dynamic, meaningful, and demanding faith enterprise. Again, "salvation" is a three-tensed thing. Good theology will be careful not to lose track of the fullness of this complex sense of time.

3. Adverbs. Adverbs are our theological answers to the many questions of the manner of faith's implementation in real life. The questions of "means" are many. Can I be a good Christian and use alcoholic beverages—didn't Jesus? If I am to live in love and with justice, may I use violence in some extreme circumstances (an unfortunate way to sometimes have to treat one's enemies)? Does the proper Christian way to dress, eat, and act shift somewhat as cultural settings shift? Can I practice homosexuality and be a good Christian?[50] These and many others are questions of *manner*, the *hows* of proper Christian living.

Do you want to be blessed by Christ in a way that leads to joyful living and effective evangelism? Did you come into this world crying while all around you were smiling? Probably. Do you now want to so live your life that, at the time of your death, all around you will be crying while you are smiling? Hopefully. Then you should be expressing your faith in this world by having your life (1) in working order, (2) properly dressed, and (3) happily expending itself in the line of Christian duty. These are the three essential *hows*.

a. In working order. Theologically speaking, how should a Christian live? To put the answer briefly, life should be lived smoothly and efficiently. This has to be done on a road full of potholes.

A fundamental fact of humanity is our *fallenness*. Something significant has happened to spoil God's creation so that it no longer works as intended. Evil has entered the picture, infecting us all—note that "evil" is "live" spelled backwards. Our functioning is disrupted. For life to work properly again there is need for God's pure and unmerited grace, a re-creation, being born again, a conversion that turns us around and sets us back in the right direction. It is nothing less than the adoption we mentioned above. Life works as it should only when we are rightly related to God.

Here's a testimony that reflects being rightly related. E. Stanley Jones titled his 1968 autobiography *A Song of Ascents*. Like the psalms of ascent sung by ancient Hebrew pilgrims as they journeyed upward toward Jerusalem (Psalms 120-134), Jones narrates his lifelong spiritual pilgrimage. At age eighty-four he still understood himself to be in the process of being formed more fully into the likeness of Jesus Christ, of being more properly related to God through Jesus. He was a Christian in-the-making, a maturing world evangelist who was focused on being Christ-preoccupied rather than self-preoccupied. To be like Christ is to have life put back in working order just as creation originally intended.

To be put in working order as Christians requires *waiting* before we start *working*. Jesus was clear that his disciples should wait before they went out to work for him in the world (Acts 1:4-5). The work to be done would put them (us) on the world's margins. The only effective way to accomplish the task was (is) to be instruments shaped and directed by the Spirit of Christ. Life in the Spirit must precede ministry through the Spirit. We can do all things that God intends when—and only when--we are divinely strengthened (Phil. 4:11-13). This strengthening, inspiring, and gifting is the work of the Spirit, the work for which we are to wait.

There is an important caution here. Our desire to do things for God can get in the way of God's desire to first do things critical for us. Theologically speaking, the most "orthodox" of believers can easily participate in "mere religion." We can be very right and all wrong. We must wait on the Spirit before we can become agents of the Spirit. We must be put in working order before we can work well for our Lord.

b. In proper dress. How should Christians live in light of their divine adoption? We are to dress properly, not to dazzle cameras and turn heads, but to reflect Jesus Christ. What do well-dressed believers look like?.

First, since we are freed from the spoilage of sin by God's gracious action, we must avoid the very appearance of evil so that we don't spoil our witness by looking like what we no longer are. As they say, we must "walk our talk" and "look the part." The Christian is to live intentionally in a way that reflects the good news come in Jesus and enabled in us by the Spirit. There is nothing attractive about a professed believer who, instead of standing consistently and courageously on the promises of God, just sits idly and selfishly on the church premises and mindlessly repeats the language and traditions of the church. Hypocrites look ridiculous and are useless!

With its first episode appearing in September, 2010, *Downton Abbey* has now gone through several seasons and become a much-loved TV series. It is about struggling to survive with the old social ways in England as the world changed around fixed standards and practices. This series is very British in its particular dress styles and social codes as they come under increased pressure for change just before, during, and after World War I.

What should last and what is only time-bound? That question always haunts Christian theology and life. For the Christian, the challenge is to model the Master, imitating Christ, carefully distinguishing between gospel *essentials* and cultural *incidentals*. The world's ground keeps shifting. Believers must stay on their feet and display something authentic that remains relevant.

This distinguishing between gospel essentials and cultural incidentals is hard work never done. For instance, decency, modesty, and the inner beauty flowing from reverence for God are always gospel essentials. But exactly what should they look like in a given social setting? This is always a question to be freshly answered. Paul identifies some essentials for how a church leader should conduct life (1 Tim. 3:2-3). He further describes in vivid imagery how believers should always be clothed in order to express the radical change that must show because of having set out on the Christian way (Gal. 3:27; Col. 3:9-10).

How should we believers dress? In nineteenth-century rural America, Christian men often refused to wear neckties because such dress tended to be viewed by the public as farmers getting ready to let off steam in town. Ties or no ties for men of Christ? It depends. Lipstick for a Christian woman is only personal preference in some settings, or in others it is sure evidence of a "loose" woman. We dare not generalize on such particulars. What we should do is put on new Christ clothes, "the whole armor of God" (Eph. 6:13-17).

Here is a good description of the spiritual clothes to be worn by every true Christian in every setting: "Divine love to all, especially to the church, the body of Christ.... Humility. . . [so that] we humble ourselves under the mighty hand of God and constantly search the scriptures to know His whole will and plan.... Living holy lives, separate from the world, the flesh and the devil, and rescuing other souls to a life of purity and holiness. There is [to be] a Holy Ghost shine on the faces of the workers."[51]

Are you dressed in this whole-armor way, the only way that helps the world see God at work and not you showing off your religion?

c. In the line of duty. How should we be living out our divine adoption? Joyfully, gratefully, and lovingly—that's how. After being changed by grace and beginning to look like it, a believer must become fruitful, acting productively like a new person in Jesus Christ should. Here is the theological agenda: have our fallenness reversed by the power of God's grace and then dress properly; and then go to work! The parable of Jesus about the "talents" says it clearly (Matt. 25). Whatever gifts you have from God, put them to work and bear fruit. I once heard this "economic" wisdom. Jesus invested his entire life in you. Have you yet earned any interest for his kingdom?

A Christian in name but not in performance is like a counterfeit dollar. It looks good but doesn't spend well. The salvation train has no sleeping cars. Salvation is by faith alone, granted, but saving faith is *never alone*—it actively works and bears fruit. Pray for a good harvest, of course, but keep hoeing while you pray. We can't earn eternal life, no matter how hard we try but, once having received such new life as a gift from God, we can keep it *only by acting like we have it*.

A central concern of the Protestant reformers of the sixteenth century (Martin Luther, John Calvin, etc.) was to motivate Christians to live their faith in the everyday world. They sought to enable Christians to involve themselves firmly in the "secular" order, bringing to public life something new and special. The home tended to replace the monastery as the primary arena where Christian life was to be focused and applied.

The home and church are to nourish believers so that they can go out into the larger world and glorify, serve, and proclaim the good news of God. To withdraw from the world is to short-circuit the current mission of eternal life. To disengage may look like one is being holy, but actually it is defaulting on what holiness is intended to be—activating the Christ-life in the world.

Salt preserves only as it permeates. To remain motionless is finally to die. Jesus made clear that true disciples are to be the light of the world, actively shining in public with the kind of life that brings glory to God (Matt. 5:14-16). A gospel chorus by Albert W. T. Orsborn expresses this well:

> Let the beauty of Jesus be seen in me—
> All His wonderful passion and purity!
> O Thou Spirit divine, All my nature refine,
> Till the beauty of Jesus be seen in me

4. Adjectives. Here is the question of appearance, the descriptions of our Christian living. If a believer is (1) in working order, (2) in proper dress, and (3) functioning fruitfully in the line of duty, what should "the world" be seeing?

We could look for the answer in Antioch. It was there that an early faith community formed around belief in Jesus as the Son of God. The result was that in this city the disciples of Jesus were first called "Christians" (Acts 11:26). That word tended to mean those followers obviously belonged to the family of Christ. They had come to reflect in their own lives the characteristics basic to who Jesus was and how and why he did things. Here are four aspects of the life of Jesus, adjectives that defined him and should now define those who faithfully follow him.

a. Community people. Maturing as a Christian believer depends in large part on being open to the community of Christ's disciples, both past and present. To be one with Christ is to seek oneness with those who are Christ's and to learn from their accumulated insight into the faith's resources and implications. To be in Christ is to be a member of his family, the church. "The

Lone Ranger" may have been a classic TV cowboy series, but it is hardly the right symbol of an appropriate Christian life. Christians should go around doing good, of course, but not in isolation, mysteriously, and behind a mask.

The church is a story-formed community of people on pilgrimage through time together, directed by the shaping force and motivating goal of the biblical story of God in Jesus Christ. The community of Christ is pictured vividly in the taking of the Lord's Supper. There is to be no more Jew/Greek, slave/free, or male/female in Christ's body. We are to "discern the body" when we eat and drink at the Lord's Table.

Salvation involves more than forgiveness of past sins. It includes the righting of relationships and the forming of a new community—the body of Christ on earth, the new Israel. To sit at the table with Christ is to be one with all who sit at the table. The church's witness to the world should be "Behold how they love!" rather than "There are divisions" (1 Cor. 11).

b. Charismatic people. Those first disciples of Jesus waited in Jerusalem as Jesus had told them to do. Then it happened, what they had been waiting for without fully realizing what was coming. It was "Pentecost," fifty days after Easter, the coming of the Spirit of Christ after the resurrection of Jesus. This event was the dramatic transition from the presence of Jesus physically in our history to the continuing presence of Christ's Spirit. That continuing divine presence is the dynamic that enables the existence of the true church and its effective life in this still-fallen world.

"Charismatic" means grace-gifts, God's way of enabling his people to be and do what God's present mission intends and demands. The charismatic tradition of Christianity celebrates the transforming and enabling that is possible in the church because of the presence and work of God's Spirit. The church is the Pentecost people on whom the Spirit's cleansing and sending power have fallen.

We cannot be God's people unless we are gifted to be the Spirit's church. If the historic events of Jesus form the past foundation of church life, the current presence of the Spirit provides the vision, energy, power, and tools for its life and ministry. We dare to hope because the triumph of goodness, grace, love, and justice does not depend ultimately on us, but on the power and work of the Spirit in and through us. The church is the gathering of the charismatic people, the saved and God-gifted people on mission together.

c. Catholic people. When you need something very basic and on short notice, go back to your A, B, Cs. Get simple and stay plain. My wife and I were in Jamaica. Without warning I was asked to address a large Christian crowd for two purposes. I was to bring "greetings" from our brothers and sisters in the United States and do it by highlighting the common theological heritage we shared in our particular church tradition. All I could think of quickly was to go basic and alphabetic.

I announced that the church should be described by three adjectives, "**a**postolic, **b**iblical, and **c**atholic." What would be easier to remember than A-B-C. I thought, and what is more appropriate for Christians than these three words? The famous Nicene Creed (381 A.D.) is a classic statement of the essential adjectives for the true church—"one, holy catholic, and apostolic." I was in a hurry in Jamaica and missed the "one." It wouldn't have fit my little alphabetic scheme anyway. My omission is an example of theology always being unfinished, done in an immediate context, never entirely whole for all time and places.

There it is, the theological A, B, Cs of church-related adjectives. "Catholic" is right in the middle. The one people of God thinks as a whole and should cover the earth. Good Christian theology is the kind that (1) stays with its original roots seen in the first apostles of Jesus (apostolic), (2) stays with teaching that fits the definitive revelation (biblical), (3) relates warmly to and serves helpfully with all of God's children (catholic), and determines to be united (one) in its learning, relating, and working. Otherwise, the witness of the church is easily seen by the world as a fragmented farce.

d. Colorful (even humorous) people. Flashy? Funny? Christians? Can you imagine Jesus bent over with a belly laugh, or causing others to do that? Well, he was accused of being something of a party animal (meals featuring questionable characters), a bit outrageous for a rabbi. He went to some of the wrong places and chatted openly with a few of the wrong people (Samaritan woman, Zacchaeus, etc.). One of my teachers wrote about the "sly humor" of Jesus, insisting that "mirth and compassion are compatible." The good news of Jesus should be freed from any "excessive sobriety."[52] Christians should relax, relate, and be truly winsome people.

Our Master was a master at using preposterous statements to make a point—have you ever see a camel trying to squeeze its humps through the eye of a needle (Mk. 10:25)? He said this to the religious leaders who were going overboard to look pious in public—"Do not look dismal!" (Matt. 6:16). Hypocrites already had all the reward they would ever get—public attention. Real religion is not parading a long face but breaking a big smile when realizing that evil, while still active, has already been defeated. The frantic activity of the lost world is only the muscles of evil jerking in the midst of their fast-coming death!

Bland and colorless Christians are tragically disconnected from their Jewish roots. The Hebrews assumed that real faith is dynamic, feeling, and celebrating. Worship was hardly limited to dreary prayer and the endless study of old books. It included dancing with the tambourine (Ps. 149:3), blowing the trumpets (Ps. 150:3), hand clapping and even shouting (Ps. 47:1). The joy of laughter burst forth when God first laid the cornerstone of the earth (Job 38:7). Israel often recalled that "when the Lord restored the fortunes of Zion. . .then our mouth was filled with laughter" (Ps. 126:1-2).

To be alive in God is to be truly alive indeed! Such aliveness should show. Salvation is the experience of being set loose to be all that God created us to be. We may become viewed by the world as "fools" (1 Cor. 1:27-30), but Christ-fools are blessed with what Paul once called *hilarotes* (English makes it "hilarity"). Believers are to give with a smile on their faces (2 Cor. 9:7) and a deep joy in their souls. We are to live and witness with an obvious and deeply abiding cheerfulness that the world does not understand—but may long for once it is seen.[53]

The disciples of John came to Jesus and asked why his disciples did not fast as they and the Pharisees did (Matt. 9:14-15). Jesus explained that the close friends of the bridegroom can hardly be grim and sad while the bridegroom is with them. Here is the message of this New Testament question and answer for today's disciples of Jesus: "It tells us that to be with Jesus is a thing of joy; it tells us that in the presence of Jesus there is a sheer, thrilling effervescence of life; it tells us that a gloom-encompassed Christianity is an impossibility. Those who walk with Christ walk in radiance of joy."[54]

When life in Christ is being lived as God intends, light appears, necessary risks are willingly taken, and hearts and doors are open. There is a oneness in the body of divinely-gifted believers. Laughter is heard and the following little prayer-song by Gloria Gaither becomes the witness of life:

> I then shall live as one who's been forgiven,
> I'll walk with joy to know my debts are paid....
> I then shall live as one who's learned compassion;
> I've been so loved that I'll risk loving, too.

> Your [God's] kingdom come around and through and in me,
> Your power and glory, let them shine through me.

Be relaxed, renewed, great company, a worthy follower of Jesus who reflected the many-faceted presence and loving compassion of God.

Good theology is good grammar. We believers are to be and to write proper theological sentences before the world. These sentences are to be established on the basic nouns and activated by the great verbs of Christ-being and Christ-doing. The noun-verb combinations are to be enlivened by the appropriate and well-placed punctuation marks, adverbs, and adjectives that glory in God's past, participate in God's present, and rest in God's fast-coming future.

14

THE END IS THE BEGINNING

Questions: Are you willing to run a race that starts at the finish line? Does that even make sense? In God's grace grammar, that which soon will be already is!

Let's begin this last chapter—which in some ways is the first—with a large and often controversial theological word, "eschatology." It's from the Greek word *eschaton*. In its narrow sense, it means a consideration of the end of all things or end-related matters (second coming of Christ, millennium, judgment, heaven, etc.). More broadly viewed, it has to do with the goal of history toward which the whole creation moves. Christian eschatology explores how creatures who have their origin in God should and can live and have their final destiny in God. In other words, the future should have a present. If what will be is crucial, so is what we are to *be* now, what we are to *be doing* in the meantime.[55]

Eschatology is not a mere addendum to theology, a description of how the whole story finally ends. Instead, it is an all-time truth that weaves its way through the warp and woof of the whole of God's story and the whole of our theology. Every major doctrine should have an eschatological aspect.[56] Jesus came not to announce the coming end of the world so much as he came to announce the dramatic fact that in his coming there had arrived the "kingdom of God" (Matt. 3:2). God glorious reign had come into the present as a grace-filled taste of God's eventual tomorrows. The long-term end was to be known by believers as a new beginning for every today!

If your interest is primarily in horoscopes, astrologers, TV soothsayers, doomsday movies, UFO sightings, and biblical signs of the times, you'll find this last chapter disappointing. Speculative eschatology of this sort was carefully avoided by Jesus, even when his disciples pushed him for what information they could get about the future and the honors they might eventually receive (Mark 10:35ff). As Jesus handled the curiosities of his disciples, our own curiosities about what lies ahead will not be satisfied here. Such a preoccupation with "inside information" about tomorrow lies outside the proper range of responsible theologians who, like Jesus, are oriented to life in Christ *now* as well as hereafter. The important thing is that the coming kingdom already has come!

The Future Is Now

Here is the central point of a properly oriented theological sentence. What *will be* for the faithful believer should be coming to real life *in the present*. To put it simply, and as Jesus did, we are to be faithful *in the meantime*. We are assured that the future lies safely in God's hands. Knowing that much of the end of God's story sets us free to participate now in what yet will be. The end is really the beginning. "Eternal" life means more than life that lasts forever. It also means a special quality of life, a life infused by the transforming presence of God. That's why every Christian doctrine should have about it something of the present-ness of God with us in Jesus Christ. He is alpha and omega, the beginning and the end. The God who will be is the same one who now is.

Where, then, are we as we approach our last chapter? When Christians are writing good sentences with their present lives (including use of the key nouns, verbs, adverbs, and adjectives of the faith), they also will be keeping their verb tenses straight. They will be putting into practice the present implications of what already has happened in Christ. They will be activating now what yet will be. The appropriate big word is *prolepsis*. We are to be assuming and representing the future as if it presently exists—which Jesus said it actually does in the life and work of the Spirit of Christ among us.

Paul raises the pivotal questions in Romans 8:33-35, concluding that no one and nothing can separate believers from the powerful love of Christ, the One who now sits at the right hand of God and ministers through the Spirit. Ephesians 1:20-21 affirms that Christ currently has complete authority. Peter gives assurance that any persecution can be endured if one is steadfast in faith (1 Peter 3:22). Here is Christian belief that sustains the faithful between the resurrection and final return of Jesus. Jesus is Lord of the between time and the end time.

By fixing our attention on the One who is the final authority over life and death, and all the history between, we learn to turn away from lives of compulsion, greed, division, and deceit (Col. 3:5-9) and instead turn toward a life of forgiveness, gratitude, and self-giving formed and enabled by divine grace. The possibility of turning toward such new life is the work of Christ's Spirit. It is to be our present joy and responsibility.

Based on biblical revelation, and according to what little we do know for sure about the future, that final tomorrow comes down to only this. Quoting the Apostles' Creed, the oldest and best-known statement of basic Christian faith, Jesus "will come again to judge the living and the dead.... I believe in the Holy Spirit...the resurrection of the body and the life everlasting." Quoting the Nicene Creed (381 A.D.), widely heralded by worldwide Christianity across so many centuries, Jesus "will come again in glory, to judge the living and the dead, and his kingdom will have no end.... We look for the resurrection of the dead, and the life of the world to come."

That's a lot to believe and hope for by faith, and it's also not much compared to what many Christians manage to come up with. They spin elaborate theories of exactly how and when and where the final days will happen and precisely what is to follow—with full detail about names, dates, and places. They see God's hand in everything around them, with the ending events equal to the morning newspaper and TV headlines. The fact is that most of that reading of the times comes from the readers and not the Bible. It's the stuff of human imagination more than biblical revelation. Theology should be robust and compelling, but also appropriately humble, restrained, and oriented to present mission more than future speculation.

Remember *Peanuts*, the beloved cartoon strip by Charles Schulz? In one cartoon strip, Linus reads from a little book to the reluctant Charlie Brown. "The way I see it, 'the cow jumped over the Moon' indicates a rise in farm prices. That part about the dish running away with the spoon must refer to the consumer." Linus then stopped reading and looked Charlie Brown right in the face. "Do you agree with me?"

Charlie Brown turns and walks away, saying something theologically significant as he goes. "I don't pretend to be a student of prophetic literature!"[57] Nor am I—or should you be. In fact, I would add, a cow jumping in the field could mean a shocking rise in farm prices, or a snake in the grass seen by a suddenly crazed cow, or a bovine convulsion caused by the poor thing not having been milked for three days—or none of the above. Our reading of current events can be a tricky business, especially when we think we see ultimate implications in the details of a story in the morning newspaper or on our favorite computer blog.

The book of Revelation that ends the New Testament is a common place for such end-time theorists to begin. In one way this book is the "Jurassic Park" of the Bible (if you have never seen this classic movie, watch it soon). This ending book of the Bible can startle the daylights out of an unsuspecting reader! Beasts of all kinds seem to be everywhere, and all seem to be after the poor little church. Even so, like my wife and I once experienced while crossing the African nation of Zambia at night—with no human-generated light existing within many miles in any direction, the deeper the darkness the brighter the stars. They were big, gleaming, everywhere up there (while dangerous animals lurked silently in the opaque vastness around us).

I dare to speak directly about the complex maze of biblical images in Revelation, this playground of speculators. The message of John to the church in this final book is actually *very simple indeed*. We enter in this book a world of code language, symbols kept secret for the safety of the persecuted saints under Roman occupation. To over-read the symbols out of context is to miss their enduring meaning and create foreign meanings. How careful we must be so that the reader finally is not the one speaking instead of the Spirit of God.

If a good sermon is supposed to have three main points, the book of Revelation wins the brevity contest. It has only two main points. Are you ready for this abbreviated sermon, the final two-point message of the Bible to believers living in this troubled and often dangerous world? Here goes. The message is as simple as it is amazing, as straightforward as it is comprehensive. It is more relevant for the present than would be details of God's final future.

Point One: Jesus is Lord of the church *now*—the challenge of surviving the present.

Point Two: Jesus also is Lord of all history and of everything beyond it—the hope that stretches *into the forever*.

That's it, all that we are sure of and that is really important. It is the big world of eschatology reduced to two simple but momentous affirmations. It's all about Jesus and his resurrection and his eternal reign.

What will be has already begun and cannot be stopped. Jesus is the ever-living and ever-reigning one. He is Alpha and Omega, the whole alphabet of reality who envelops all the tenses of our faith and originates all the adverbs and adjectives that should characterize the lives of his followers. He is present assurance and future fulfillment. He is Lord of lords and King of kings, those of the present and of any other time to come. Knowing this and being assured by this, we are to relax and get to work!

We all know that problems persist—for now. Kings are arrogant, yes, but Jesus is the ruler of the kings! The world is still in turmoil, yes, but the Book of Revelation begins and ends with "the grace of Jesus." There is hope for now and later! It's God's church. John knew this. Since evil had not defeated Jesus on the cross, the cross being experienced by the church would find its own resurrection by the same power! The new life in Jesus is indeed eternal in nature, God's kind of resurrection life that reflects the life of God and thus has no ending.

This book of John's ends the whole Bible with a "hallelujah chorus"—and "they shall reign for ever and ever" (22:5). No matter what comes in the meantime, the victory is the Lord's! The book also carries warnings for life in the meantime, for those who first read the scroll soon after it got off the island of Patmos and for those like you and me who read it only now.

Wake up and stay faithful! The book tells us not to compromise in order to fit into a pagan world. Wake up and believe! Rome is a beast that takes its power from Satan, receives worship that belongs only to God, and has no future (Rev. 13). Wake up and know this! This human city and its temporary empire are full of violence and idolatry and God is about to call it to judgment. Wake up and be assured! Judgment is coming because God always will reign supreme. Be steady and full of hope, and stay in working order. The future is yours. It is sure and not far away.

Did you get the two-part message? Here is another way to express it. When it comes to theology, a little poetry is always a good thing.

> The future lies unseen ahead, It holds I know not what;
> But still I know I need not dread, For Jesus fails me not.
> The glory of eternal dawn, Shines from His smiling face;
> So, trusting Him, I follow on, With heart made strong by grace.
> I'll follow Him with rejoicing, With rejoicing, rejoicing;
> I know He safely will lead me, To my eternal home.[58]

It's as simple and wonderful as that. The two-point message? Jesus is Lord *now* and *then*. "I saw a Great White Throne and the One Enthroned. Nothing could stand before or against the Presence, nothing in heaven, nothing on earth" (Rev. 20:11, *The Message*).

Here's a fundamental fact not to be missed as Christian theology is done in any generation. The fact is as profound as it is simple. It wasn't nails that held Jesus to the cross—it was love! It isn't evil that eventually will remain, but love, God's love. "And now faith, hope, and love abide, these three; and the greatest of these is love" (1 Cor. 13:13).

If this is so, what then should believers in Jesus be doing in the present, troubled as it might be? "Let evildoers do their worst and the dirty-minded go all out in pollution, but let the righteous maintain a straight course and the holy continue on in holiness" (Rev. 22:11, *The Message*).

Ending Without Finishing

When does the work of theology come to an end? The simple answer is "never," at least not while time lasts. We never will have it all just right, never understand fully the things of God, never have the final answers to the biggest questions (like the presence of evil in God's world). We never will have the privilege of living and thinking in a stable social setting where language is fixed and Christ-like values are shared. There is always more theological work to be done.

This ongoing aspect of theological work can be seen in the titles of some published stories of a few theologians. My own life story is titled *A Pilgrim's Progress*. The one by James Earl Massey is titled *Aspects of My Pilgrimage*. My biography of Clark H. Pinnock is titled *Journey Toward Renewal*. Malcolm Muggeridge's autobiography is titled *Confessions of a Twentieth-Century Pilgrim*. We all have known constant movement and learned that doing the work of Christian theology is a never-ending business. Ponder these words of Muggeridge:

How to fit together the pieces of this cosmic jigsaw puzzle? The passing moments of a life in the setting of Eternity; the tiny planet Earth in the setting of the Universe; a loving God who has counted the hairs of all our heads, who cannot see a sparrow fall to the ground without concern, and the wild, ferocious story of mankind—civilizations that come and go, leaving their debris behind them for archaeologists to dig and diagnose; wars that are won and lost; philosophers who are credible and then scorned; today's beliefs, tomorrow's folly; today's hero, tomorrow's villain or idiot; Towers of Babel everlastingly being built and never finished.[59]

That should be enough to humble us all as we do our thing in the passing moments that we are on life's stage. But with the reality of never being adequate or finished comes some really good news. The God who first called us to the journey also walks by our sides, showing us the right path, promising to lead us all the way home. So, in the middle of whatever troubles us now, our hearts can still cry out, "Thanks be to God!"

Another theologian gives wisdom we need. Karl Barth is clearly one of the greats in the world of Christian theology. His *Church Dogmatics* is a huge and immensely respected life's work (some 9,000 pages in German!). Late in life he was asked if he intended to add to this extensive production--already possibly the longest systematic theology ever written. He said, "probably not. I already have written more than enough for people to read." When anyone would inquire about another volume being added, he would ask if they had finished reading carefully the first twelve--rarely had anyone, even his greatest admirers.

Barth compared his theological work to the great Strasbourg Cathedral in France. It had only one tower even though its building plan had called for two. Said Barth, "There is a certain merit to an unfinished dogmatics. It points to the eschatological character of theology."[60] There is that "eschatology" word again. What Barth meant was that his many theological words only glimpsed what still lies ahead in time and always exists beyond human comprehension. His theology speaks substantially of the ultimate without itself being ultimate. He was known to say that his theology was written in Basel, Switzerland, not in heaven. Even so, he knew—and so should we—that heaven has already come to us and wants to permeate all that we now are and do.

All theologies, this one included, are written somewhere other than in heaven. If they are good theologies, they are driven by and filled with the heaven that already has come to us. They radiate the special grammar of God's saving grace. They are very important, but never finished, never the final word while time shall last.

So I end here, having said more than enough to help you write good theological sentences. I end, as does all theological work, without finishing.

Endnotes

[1] See Barry L. Callen, *Heart of the Matter* (Emeth Press, 2011).

[2] See Walter Brueggemann, "The Power of Dreams in the Bible," *Christian Century* (June 28, 2005), 28-31.

[3] Frederick Buechner, *Peculiar Treasures* (HarperSanFrancisco, 1979), 90.

[4] Buechner, 20.

[5] John Killinger, *You Are What You Believe: The Apostles' Creed for Today* (Abingdon Press, 1990).

[6] Alister McGrath, *Understanding Doctrine* (Zondervan, 1990), 2-5.

[7] Ambrose Bierce, *The Devil's Dictionary* (N.Y.: Dover Publications, 1958), 65.

[8] Stanley Hauerwas and William Willimon, *Resident Aliens: Life in the Christian Colony* (Abingdon Press, 1989), 164-165.

[9] Barry L. Callen, *Caught Between Truths: The Central Paradoxes of Christian Faith* (Emeth Press, 2007), 55.

[10] See D. Lyle Dabney, "Jürgen Moltmann and John Wesley's Third Article Theology" in the *Wesleyan Theological Journal*, Spring/Fall, 1994, 140ff; Clark Pinnock, *Flame of Love: A Theology of the Holy Spirit* (InterVarsity Press, 1996).

[11] Callen, *Caught Between Truths*, 28.

[12] Barry L. Callen, *God As Loving Grace* (1996), *Radical Christianity* (1999), *Discerning the Divine* (2004), *Caught Between Truths* (2007), and *Heart of the Matter* (2011).

[13] These novels of mine were published in 2010, 2011, and 2009 respectively.

[14] Stanley J. Grenz and Roger E. Olson, *Who Needs Theology?* (InterVarsity Press, 1996).

[15] Grenz/Olson, op. cit., 67.

[16] Quoted in the *Christian Science Monitor* (October 21, 2013), 6.

[17] Helmut Thielicke, *A Little Exercise for Young Theologians* (Eerdmans Publishing, 1962), 3.

[18] Ibid., 37.

[19] Ibid., 36-37.

[20] Stanley Hauerwas and William H. Willimon, *Resident Aliens: Life in the Christian Colony* (Abingdon Press, 1989), 165.

[21] Thielicke, op. cit., 81.

[22] Kevin Mannoia, *Masterful Living: New Vocabulary for the Holy Life*, rev. ed. (Aldersgate Press, 2012).

[23] Brian D. McLaren, *Naked Spirituality: A Life with God in 12 Simple Words* (HarperOne, 2011), 73.

[24] McLaren, op. cit., 18.

[25] Laurie H. DuBose, "'Tis Then," *Alliance Life* (formerly *Alliance Witness*), June 6, 1984. This is the official magazine of the Christian and Missionary Alliance church.

[26] Boyce W. Blackwelder, *Light from the Greek New Testament* (Warner Press, 1958), 30.

[27] My process preference does not wholly adopt what often today is called "process theology." While full of valuable insights, I judge this school of theological thought to be too light on certain biblically-defined nouns, especially God being truly sovereign in the sense of existing prior to the creation and being independent of even while deeply involved in the creation.

[28] Peter Elbow, *Vernacular Eloquence: What Speech Can Bring to Writing* (2012).

[29] Leonard Sweet, *Out of the Question...Into the Mystery* (Waterbrook Press, 2004), 55.

[30] Stanley Grenz, reported in Grenz and Olson, *op. cit.*, 75.

[31] Stanley J. Grenz and Roger E. Olson, *Who Needs Theology?* (InterVarsity Press, 1996), 10.

[32] Stanley J. Grenz and Roger E. Olson, *20th-Century Theology: God & the World in a Transitional Age* (InterVarsity Press, 1992).

[33] See Barry L. Callen, *Caught Between Truths: The Central Paradoxes of Christian Faith* (Lexington, KY: Emeth Press, 2007).

[34] David Ray Griffin, *God & Religion in the Postmodern World* (State University of New York Press, 1989), 1.

[35] John Meyendorff, *Orthodoxy and Catholicity* (N.Y.: Sheed and Ward, 1966), 133-134.

[36] Bishop Kallistos Ware, *The Orthodox Way* (Crestwood, N.Y.: St. Vladimir's Seminary Press, rev. ed., 1999), 14-17.

[37] Randy L. Maddox, "John Wesley and Eastern Orthodoxy," *Asbury Theological Journal* 45:2 (Fall 1990), 29-53.

[38] See another Western theologian, Emil Brunner, and his book *Truth as Encounter* (London: SCM, rev. ed., 1964).

[39] Daniel B. Clendenin, *Eastern Orthodox Christianity: A Western Perspective* (Grand Rapids: Baker Books, 1994), 53. Emphasis added.

[40] Paul Tillich, Systematic Theology, vol. 1, 1951, 3.

[41] President John A. Morrison of Anderson University, in *Alumni News* (February, 1957).

[42] Barry L. Callen, *Authentic Spirituality: Moving Beyond Mere Religion* (Emeth Press, 2006), 19.

[43] Clark H. Pinnock, *Most Moved Mover: A Theology of God's Openness* (Baker Academic, 2001), 5-6.

[44] From the Journal of John Wesley, entry for May 24, 1738, emphasis added.

[45] See an elaboration of all this in Callen, *Authentic Spirituality*, 85-88.

[46] Marvin R. Wilson, *Our Father Abraham: Jewish Roots of the Christian Faith* (Eerdmans and Center for Judaic-Christian Studies, 1989), 136.

[47] See these root metaphors elaborated in Richard B. Hays, *The Moral Vision of the New Testament* (HarperSanFrancisco, 1996).

[48] Martin Luther King, Jr., as quoted by Wayne Phillips, "Negroes Pledge to Keep Boycott," *New York Times*, 24 February, 1956, 8.

[49] Jon Meacham, "Pilgrim's Progress," *Newsweek* (August 14, 2006), 43.

[50] For a brief but careful treatment of his very controversial question, see Howard Snyder, *Homosexuality and the Church* (Asbury Seminary: Seedbed, 2014).

[51] William J. Seymour, "Marks of Fanaticism," *The Apostolic Faith* 1, no. 2 (1906), 2.

[52] D. Elton Trueblood, *The Humor of Christ* (Harper & Row, 1964), 22, 10.

[53] Several dimensions of this "hilarious" Christian life are explored in the Nov./Dec. 1994 issue of the Christian spiritual journal called *Weavings*.

[54] William Barclay, *The New Daily Study Bible*, Matthew, vol. 1 (Westminster John Knox, 2001 ed.), 388.

[55] For a full treatment of this important truth, the present-ness of God's future, see Barry L. Callen, *Faithful in the Meantime* (Evangel Publishing, 1997).

[56] H. Ray Dunning, *Grace, Faith, and Holiness: A Wesleyan Systematic Theology* (Beacon Hill Press of Kansas City, 1988), 13.

[57] Robert L. Short, *The Gospel According to Peanuts* (Westminster John Knox Press, 1999), 24.

[58] Verses one and four and the chorus of "I'll Follow with Rejoicing" by Charles W. Naylor and Andrew L. Byers.

[59] Malcolm Muggeridge, *Confessions of a Twentieth-Century Pilgrim* (San Francisco: Harper & Row, 1988), 52-53.

[60] John Godsey, *Karl Barth: How I Changed My Mind* (John Knox Press, 1966), 86.

www.ingramcontent.com/pod-product-compliance
Lightning Source LLC
Chambersburg PA
CBHW031316150426
43191CB00005B/252